Joseph William Reynolds

The mystery of Miracles

Joseph William Reynolds

The mystery of Miracles

ISBN/EAN: 9783743305649

Manufactured in Europe, USA, Canada, Australia, Japa

Cover: Foto ©ninafisch / pixelio.de

Manufactured and distributed by brebook publishing software (www.brebook.com)

Joseph William Reynolds

The mystery of Miracles

THE
MYSTERY OF MIRACLES

The unity of the natural and the supernatural is proved by the teleological design of nature to subserve the Kingdom of God; and by a capacity of progress which manifests continuance of transcendental activity in the course of worlds.

Nature is not a hindrance to freedom, it is rather the organ of freedom; and, in Miracles, freedom is exercised by power coming from a free Creator.

THE
MYSTERY OF MIRACLES

BY THE AUTHOR

OF

"THE SUPERNATURAL IN NATURE"

LONDON
C. KEGAN PAUL & CO. 1 PATERNOSTER SQUARE
1879

Authority is that which, reason and experience having sanctioned, common acceptation commends.

Science is the sum total of verified or verifiable knowledge.

With every increase of intelligence and healthful growth of knowledge is a corresponding enlargement as to the realities and possibilities of clear-headed and true-hearted belief.

THE MYSTERY OF MIRACLES.

RESPECTFULLY DEDICATED TO SCIENTIFIC MEN.

IN ENDEAVOURING TO GIVE
GENERALIZATION AND EMBODIMENT TO THE GREAT TRUTHS
WHICH HAVE BEEN SOUGHT WITH SO MUCH TOIL,
AND EXHIBITED WITH SUCH FIDELITY AND SKILL,
BY SCIENTIFIC STUDENTS ;
THE AIM HAS BEEN TO
PRESENT THOSE TRUTHS AS COUNTERPART AND EVIDENCE OF MIRACLES,
THAT WE MAY
JOIN MORE READILY IN COMMON SERVICE OF THE GREAT MASTER,
AND GATHER MORE HAPPILY
INTO ONE FAMILY AS CHILDREN OF GOD.

THE AUTHOR.

VERITAS MAXIMA CARITAS.

CONTENTS.

HOW AND WHY I THOUGHT.

	PAGE
The Thing to be Done	1
Union of Reason and Faith Enlarges the Man	2
Reason and Faith are Wedded	3
They Elevate the Meaning of Scripture and Enlarge our Thought as to the Work of Nature	3
Great and Strange Things to be Looked for	4
Germ of the Present Conception	5
View of Molecular Movement	5
Coming of Life without Observation	6
Beginning of Animal Existence	6
Consummation in Man	7
The Developed Thought	7
Time that we add Faith to Science and Culture	8

THOUGHT I.

THE DENIAL OF MIRACLES IS UNSCIENTIFIC.

Cannot be Maintained	10
A Guessing at the Unknown	11
The Error as to God and Nature	11
A Little wherewith to Measure the Great	12
Nature Derivative	13

THOUGHT II.

NATURALISM AND SUPERNATURALISM.

	PAGE
Naturalism Convicted of Inadequacy	14
Right View of Naturalism	15
Supernaturalism as opposed to Naturalism	16
Two Sides of Existence	16
Illustrated by Crystallization	17
Architectural Energy	17
The First Beginning	17
Many Beginnings	18
Science Reveals a Progressive Kingdom	19

THOUGHT III.

INNER IMPULSE TO THE MIRACULOUS.

Peace and Surety of High Faith	21
Nature a Garment of the Unseen	21
Mental Marvels possess Reality	22
No Mental Miracles if the Physical are Impossible	22
Argument on Unequal Feet	23
Mystery Everywhere	23

THOUGHT IV.

WORLD WITHIN THE WORLD.

Belief and Will	25
Belief in Miracles not a Delusion	25
Based on Realities	26
An Inner World	27
Two Faces	27
The Keys and Anthem of Intellect	27
Life and Mental Action in Diminutive Degree	28
Eternity of Matter a Marvel	28
Creation of Matter a Miracle	29
The Process Wonderful	29

THOUGHT V.

HIDDEN THINGS.

	PAGE
Our Position	31
Spirit Looks through our Thinking	32
Inwardness and Knitted Purport	32
Knowing the Unknown	33
Minuteness and Gradation	34
Principles at Work and Progress of Life	34
A Sixth Sense, Insight	36
Imaginary Quantities	36
Practical Conclusions	37
Matter and Energy from the Unseen	38

THOUGHT VI.

ARE MIRACLES IMPROBABLE?

They are not Improbable	40
Miracles Associated with Imperishable Wisdom	40
Improbability of the Improbability	41
True Idea of a Miracle	41
Everything passes into the Miraculous	42
The Process of Advance Miraculous	42
The Advance could not be Foreseen	43
Vain Effort to Explain away the Marvel	43
Progress not without Direction and Heart of Reason	44

THOUGHT VII.

IS BELIEF IN MIRACLES UNREASONABLE?

Antiquity the Home of the Supernatural	46
Statement of Locke	46
,, ,, Spinosa	47
,, ,, Neander	47
Miracles are Signs and Tests of Faith	47
Miraculous Deeds in Connection with Miraculous Words	47
Natural Processes are Akin to the Supernatural	49
Outer Signs of the Inner and Spiritual	49
Linking and Blending of the Two Miraculous	50

	PAGE
Unconscious Activity of Reason in Nature	51
Thought as to Flowers	51
Something within Ourselves and Nature that exceeds Both	52
The whole World Contemporaneous	53
This Physical Truth has Spiritual Reality	54
Nature Borders on the Supernatural	54

THOUGHT VIII.

ARE MIRACLES UNNATURAL?

The Natural Arises from the Supernatural	56
The Miraculous not more Supernatural than is Nature	56
The Scenes of Nature are Moved by an Invisible Power	57
Antecedents and Consequents not Visibly Tied	57
End of the World	58
Order of Nature	59
No Power of Causation in Nature	59
The Miracle a Mark of a Superinduced Nature	60
Inability to Explain Miracles Scientifically is no Reason for Refusal	60
The Known Course of Nature not the only Course	61

THOUGHT IX.

COSMICAL AND MENTAL ANALOGIES.

Nature Presents Strange Combinations	63
Suspension of Gravity	63
Isomerism	64
Electricity and Magnetism	64
Examples by Fire	65
Changes in the Nature of Things	65
Phosphorus	65
Oxygen	65
Sulphur	65
Allotropism	65
Falling Stones and Meteors	66
Chemical Combinations	67

Contents. xi

	PAGE
Unexpected Varieties	67
The Same Substances in Different States	68
Vital and Mental Processes	69
Miracles Explained by an Inner Sense	70
Few Truths Known Mightily	71

THOUGHT X.
MIRACLES ARE CREDIBLE.

Hume's Statement is False	72
The Statement Varied	73
Threefold Fallacy	73
Miracles Established by Experience	74
The Natural not Miraculous	74
The Moral Argument	75
The Fallacy of Inexperience Displayed	75
Existence of Miracles a Lesser Marvel than their Non-Existence	76
General Conviction of the Miraculous	76
Separation of True from False Miracles	76
Scripture and Miracles are not Inventions	77
Miracles are Sign-Manuals of Doctrine	77
Connected with People who are an Enigma	79
Accept the Lesser Miracle that there are Miracles	80

THOUGHT XI.
MIRACLES ARE CAPABLE OF PROOF.

Assertion—A Miracle cannot be Proved	81
Profane Statement	81
Disproved	82
Course of Nature full of Marvels	82
Knowing of God	83
Argument as to Cause and Effect	83
Series of Verifications	85
Perverted Argument concerning Laws	86
Reversal of the Statement	86
Verification by Example	87
Variety underlying Laws	87
Example of Deviation	87
Physicists not Omnipresent	88
Derivative Origin of Nature	89
Existence of Modification and of Variety	91

THOUGHT XII.

THE UNIVERSE A COMPLEMENT OF INTELLECT.

	PAGE
The Order of it Intellectual	92
Matter of the Earth—Used and Unused	92
Nature does not Create	92
The World Exists in Time	93
Force acting in a Straight Line incompetent to Create other Movements	93
Primal Matter, Destitute of Properties, could not, of itself, give Form and Motion to the Universe	94
Formative Power	94
Forces of Nature	95
Mechanical and Volitional Operation	96
The Universe an Organism	96
One Principle in all the Complexity and Variety	97
The Process of Reasoning Reversed	97
Man a Symbol	98
The World in Connection with a Sublime Teleology	98
Divine Interference not a Mark of Weakness but a Means of Variety	99

THOUGHT XIII.

AUTOMATISM.

Spontaneousness of Nature	100
Verification of Miracles	100
Thought as we View the Sky	101
Events Succeeding at Random	101
Luminosity of Photogenic Structures	102
Casting off of Limbs by Invertebrates	103
Unconscious Reason of Nature is a Transcendental Influence	103
Visible Existence rooted in the Invisible	105
Meaning of Automatism	105
Automatism of Nature a Co-operation with God	106

THOUGHT XIV.

SYMBOLS.

Nature's Hieroglyphs	107
Space leads to Idea of Infinitude	107
Space occupied by Æther	107

Contents.

	PAGE
Adjustment of Forces and of Individuality	107
Germ of Sense of Responsibility	108
Means of Liberty	108
Every Event, taken by itself, is Unnatural	108
Germs of Life	109
Undetectable Conditions	109
Organic Cells	109
Letters of an Unknown Language—Origin of Evil	110
Common Natural Events, standing alone, would be Incredible	111
They are Parts of a Great System	111
The Whole under Law	112
Artistic Nature	113
Symbol of a Miracle	113
By Intelligence we bring Structural Power into Operation	114
Ameliorative Process in the Earth	114
No Rock Barrier between the Natural and the Supernatural	115
Disproof of Statement against the Evidence for Miracles	115
Reversal of Statement as to Meaning of Marvellous Events	115
Any Event contrary to Law possible only by Divine Power	116
Mysterious Action is Discerned	116
Qualifying and Magnifying of Experiences	116
Experiment with Tuning Forks	117
Inner Potentialities	118
The World full of Divinity	118

THOUGHT XV.
GROUPING OF MIRACLES.

Changes are Continuance in another Form	120
With Matter so with Mind, God does not Unmake His Works	120
The First Group of Miracles	121
Our Grand System of Life	121
The Process of Advance	122
The Second Group of Miracles	123
Those of the New Testament	124
A Familiar Example—the Bee	124
Stress laid by our Lord and the Apostles on Miracles	126

THOUGHT XVI.
SPIRITUAL INSIGHT.

Advance of Inductive Science	127
Living for Both Worlds	127

	PAGE
Miracles to be Viewed on Two Sides	128
Miracles Viewed on the Side of Nature	128
Miracles Viewed on the Side of Spirit	128
False View of Quantity as to Miracles	129
Difficulty same as that attending the Use of any other Power	129
Physical Evil is the Embodiment of Spiritual Evil	130
Further View	130
Optic Nerve and Rays of Light	131
Experiments—Clouds of the Sky	131
By Light of Natural Wonders Discern other Marvels	132
Verification by the Thoughtful as a Touch of Nature by Divinity	133

THOUGHT XVII.

ACTION OF SPIRIT ON MATTER.

The Natural in Subordination to the Spiritual	134
Medium for Action of Spirit on Matter	135
Possibility of Direct Action	135
Thought, Fiction, Belief	135
Possibility of Many Media	136
Physical Phenomena are Transformations of Motion	138
Mental Action Presents Two Faces	138*
Synthesis of Consciousness	139
Links between Mind and Matter Unknown	139
Influence of Will	139
Mental States produce Physical Effects	139
Thought-Reading	140
Raising of present Human Powers would Effectuate Marvels	141

THOUGHT XVIII.

DWARFED MEN.

Miracles the Proper Evidence of Christianity	142
Dwarfing of Men	142
Blinding of Men	142
Worst Kind of Diminishment	143
Self-limiting to the Brute Sensual Range	143

	PAGE
The Low cannot Comprehend the High	144
The Dwarfed Life, at the Best, not worth Living	145
Vegetal Human Germs	146
The Fleshly Progression	147
Animal Kingdom likened to a Tree	147
Disappearance of Difference	147
The Kith of Man	148
Hypothesis of Advance—Our Duty	148

THOUGHT XIX.

MECHANICAL VIEW OF THE WORLD.

Mere Mechanism cannot be Self-Existing	150
The World as a Building	150
The World as a Tree	151
The Universe Unique	151
I. Materialistic Hypothesis—The World a Perpetual Motion	151
Refutation	152
Otherwise Expressed	153
II. Materialistic Hypothesis—Progression by Mechanical Force	153
Refutation	153
Progression from No Life to Life—Unknown	154
Not by unaided Automatism	156
III. Materialistic Hypothesis—All Forces are Mechanical	157
Refutation	157
The Mechanical Theory Inadequate	157
Matter and Inertia	158
Recognition of the Deity	158
The Universe of Divine Workmanship	159

THOUGHT XX.

KNOWLEDGE COMES BUT WISDOM LINGERS.

Knowledge and Wisdom	161
Inaccurate Statement as to Water	162
Inaccuracy as to Protoplasm	163
Unity of Life Contains Variety of Germs	163

xvi *Contents.*

	PAGE
Variation Due to Inner and Outer Force	164
No Example of Spontaneous Generation	164
Plan revealed by Evolution Wonderful	165
A Simple View of the Process	166
Confounding of Material and Mental Properties	166
Straying of Knowledge as to Sensation and Mental Activity	167
Correlation of Forces	168
Energy of an Organism in its every Part	169
Building and Blending of Matter, of Life, of Intelligence	170
Nature of Mind not essentially Material	172
Our Consciousness rests on Something Permanent	172
Connection with other States of Being	172
Evidence of an All-pervading Substance	173
Wisdom Better than Knowledge	173
An Inner Electric Telegraph	174

THOUGHT XXI.

HUMAN-WISE.

Reproach of Anthropomorphism	175
Low Anthropomorphism	175
Error as to Man	176
Error as to God	176
Maximum Finite Brain	177
True Anthropomorphism	177
Spiritual Image and Worship of God	178
Embodiment of Worship in Christ	178
Personality and Infinity not Incompatible	179
Personality the Highest Form of Being	179

THOUGHT XXII.

LAW WITHIN THE LAW.

Divine Personal Government	181
Being and Existence	181
Maintenance of Government	182
Science of Mechanism Applied	182

	PAGE
Æthereal Influx	182
Influence of Will on Matter	182
Media and Form	183
Form in Higher Sense	183
Building up of Form	183
Character of Form	184
Rising to Things Spiritual and Divine	184
Working of a Plan in Order and Affinity	185
Plan is the Enabling Power of Foresight	185
Fixity and Unfixity and Freedom	186
What is the Soul to the Body?	186
Identity and Unity	187
Correspondence, Inner and Outward	187
Automatic and Volitional Arcs	188
The Contrast	188
Controlling Power acting by Volitional Arcs	189
Abuse and Use of the Controlling Power	189
Formation of Character	190
Local Abode of Faculties	190
Spiritual Energy of Volitional Arcs	191
Acquisition of Energy	191
Mental Training—Selective Attention	192
Moral Selective Attention	192
Exercise of Control—Responsibility	193
Freedom a Fact	193
Foreknowledge of this Freedom	194
Interposition of Remedy for Evil	194
Divine Persuasion to Good	195

THOUGHT XXIII.

EVOLUTION AS A TRUE THEORY.

Evolution a Divine Process	197
The Universe is Manifold	198
Narrowness of Materialist	198
Difficulty of the Believer Removed	198
Progress from the Unseen and Past connected with a Spiritual Unseen	199
Our God-consciousness and Immortality	199
Our Conception of Godhead Finite and Imperfect	200

xviii *Contents.*

	PAGE
The Limited and Conditioned are connected with Infinity and Eternity	201
Is Matter Eternal?	201
Development of Matter	202
Development of Life	202
Life only from Life	203
Science and the Prophets' Book	203
The Bible a Progressive Revelation	204
Spiritualities are the Great Realities	205
Our Spiritual Education	206
Old Miracles live on in the Truths they attested	206
Evolving of Higher Nature by Spiritual Processes	207

THOUGHT XXIV.

LIGHT OF NATURE.

Nature Manifests the Unknown	209
Revelation of Divinity	209
Man Endowed with other Attributes than those of Matter	210
The Universe a Work of Skill	210
A Divine Kingdom within Nature	211
The Spirit that by which we View God	212
Premonitions of Future Powers	212
Relation to That Beyond and Above Nature	213
Man a Citizen of Two Cities	213
Analogies	214
Peculiarity of Position and Duality of Nature	214
Linked Purpose Unites the Whole	214
Miracles are Master Works	215
Evil and Waste turned to Good and Use	216

THOUGHT XXV.

THE GOD-MAN.

Great Men make the History of Mankind	217
Are Great in Themselves	217
Great Men are a Power Subduing Nature	218
The Hero a Man of Faith	218

	PAGE
Men who are never Great	219
The Sceptic Incomplete	219
A Great Man is a God-Man	220
Represents in Nature That which is Beyond Nature	220
Greatness and Self-Sacrifice	221
Divine Humanity—Christ	221
Incarnation affirms two Truths	222
Christ not a Creature of Time	223
The God-Man not an Evolution	223
Jesus Christ a Mystery and Greatest of our Race	224
Christly Men	224
Many Worlds and Many Sorts	225
Law Everywhere—not Uniformity	226
Man hath Sinned and God hath Suffered	227
Progress and Triumph of Humanity	227
A Coming Salvation explains the Mystery of Creation	228
Creation to be Viewed from the Highest Point	228
Jesus the Original Thinker	229
Advent of Jesus Foretold	229
Maketh all the World Akin	230
True King of the Human Kingdom	230
In Christ is our Life	230
His Coming Dominion	231
Effectuation by the Word of God	232
Light and Power by Christ	232

THOUGHT XXVI.

RESPICE, ASPICE, PROSPICE.

Looking Back	235
Looking Around	235
Looking Forward	236
Steps of Ascent to the Heights—Miracles	237
Faith is the Mark of High Intelligence	237
Forged Miracles	238
Purpose of Miracles as to the Jews	239
All Marvels are antecedently Incredible	240
I. Miracles as to Evil and Error	240
A Means of Teaching and of Strength	241
The Place of Miracles in Scripture	242
Satanic Miracles	242

	PAGE
II. Miracles as to Righteousness and Truth	243
Universality of Plan	244
Wonderfulness of Doctrine	244
Elevating Power of the Precepts	245
Affirmation of Miracles	245

THOUGHT XXVII.

ONE MIRACLE MORE.

Scepticism a Fatal Misery	247
The Men to be Raised	247
The Power they Receive	249
The Earth a Spiritual Harvest-Field	249
The Present a Ground-Plan or Preparation	250
The Natural Person becomes a Spiritual Person	251
How the Christly Process is Hindered	252
Jewish Unbelief a Mystery	253
Hindrance by Spiritual Evil	254
Evil not an Essential Part of the Divine Plan	255
The One Miracle More—	
A Glorification of Nature	256
A Glorification of Life	256
A Glorification of Intelligence	256
What the Mystery of Miracles Accomplishes	260

THE MYSTERY OF MIRACLES.

HOW AND WHY I THOUGHT.

"Crede mihi non est parvæ fiduciæ, polliceri opem decertantibus, consilium dubiis, lumen cæcis, spem dejectis, refrigerium fessis. Magna quidem hæc sunt, si fiant; parva, si promittantur. Verum ego non tam aliis legem ponam, quam legem vobis meæ propriæ mentis exponam: quam quis probaverit, teneat; cui non placuerit, abjiciat. Optarem, fateor, talis esse, qui prodesse possim quamplurimis."*

PETRARCH, *De Vita Solitaria*.

My former work, "The Supernatural in Nature," gave a general yet actual verification of miracles such as cannot be weakened unless most of our present science is proved to be inaccurate. That verification, however, owing to comprehensiveness of the argument, could not combine scientific precision with great brevity; and I

---

* Believe me, it requireth no little confidence to promise help to the struggling, advice to the doubtful, light to the blind, hope to the dejected, refreshment to the weary. These indeed are great things, if done: trifles, if only promised. I, however, do not so much prescribe a law to others; as of my own mind set forth a law: which, let him who shall approve, abide by; and let him, who approveth not, reject. I confess that I could wish to be such an one as might benefit as many as possible.

have been urged to give in a new form, separate from any special verification of Holy Scripture, and, so far as may be practicable, a concise yet adequate proof of miraculous operation in the world: operation sometimes effectuated by use of, so called, natural means; sometimes without any apparent means whatever. I respectfully present these Thoughts as helpful towards the scientific and philosophical solution of a problem which has long perplexed many minds. I endeavour to show that mystery and miracle are the source and foundation of nature, underlie all science, are everywhere and interpenetrate all things: that the abnormal and eccentric are not only possible but probable and actual, having counterparts in marvels of human consciousness, being represented by many natural symbols, and exhibited day by day in the interactions, co-operations, and counteractions of cosmic energies.

For a considerable period, fear existed in the common mind that clear, calm, accurate thinking, high capacity and attainment in pure science, not only hindered spiritual worship; but rendered men of grand intelligence actually incapable of the child-like faith and reverence so continually enforced in Holy Scripture. This fear is now passing away. Truly scientific men are growing in assurance that there is no great chasm between Reason and Faith. Highest reason and purest faith may unite in the same intellect, and light spring from each for the guidance of both; their combined brightness being the illumination of a perfect man. Possessors of science are not narrowed, with souls only in the bud; nor do they so contract natural laws as to leave no room in the universe for superphysical energies.

They behold nature as the outer form of inner powers —the material habitation for many existences—the clock to strike hours, and the pendulum to measure space for intelligences—the school for faith, patience, and discernment—where man awakes in moral stage to possess immortal being.

The most capable of our Theologians know equally well that Reason and Faith are wedded by Divine ordinance, and that divorce were a shame to both. Faith not only possesses the grandeur of Jacob's ladder by which we climb to Heaven, but is a staff for our walk on earth withal. Reason, not only doorkeeper in the House of God, but guide to things within the veil, explains the difference between sobriety and madness, between fools and wise.

When reason and faith are thus united in a man, when purest science and child-like trust combine in the same intellect; piety, knowing that her face shines most pleasantly in pure and clear light, kindles the golden lamp of her life at the bright flame of intelligence. Holy Scripture ceases to be an imperfect manuscript, with broken periods and letters effaced; and Nature is no more a barren land—every bush gleams with light— every garden is a paradise. Sparks of knowledge, struck out by the smiting of our intellect on the hard things of existence, are not the enflamed aspirations of a beast; nor the light of dead men; nor the surviving ghostly thoughts of former generations; but that scintillation, arising from spiritual potentiality of heat and light which leads high natures to acquaintance with truth, and conducts a pure conscience to the illumination of righteousness.

Whether Theologians, or Students of Science, we are aware that our age is the era of great discoveries; and, probably, the eve of astounding marvels. If the phonograph, the spectroscope, the electric light, are given; why cannot water be made an available fuel, and the refuse of coal-tar be converted into quinine? Seeing that we already manufacture various gems well-nigh undistinguishable from those of Nature; why should not some chemist discover the secret of making the diamond, and the dream of alchemists be realized that lead may be turned into gold—from which it seems to differ less than iron-ore from Whitworth's compressed steel? All these, and yet greater discoveries, would not be miracles; but they show that even the strange old bundles of superstitions were not merely bindings of error. We look for things yet stranger: that even unbelievers will discern, from feelings at work in their own heart, how the intensity of passion and truth in the bosom of Brutus enabled him to behold a mysterious vision on the eve of the notable battle of Philippi; and learn, by sins and sorrows of their own, to understand how, even if the Witch of Endor cannot bring a Samuel from the spirit-land, Saul may, nevertheless, in the subjectiveness and abjectness of his own mind, see spectres and hear messages from the great deep. Whosoever attains the true likeness and dignity of men, will understand that there are many realms in nature; and, though the whole are not sufficient habitation to contain Infinitude, the Almighty abides in the world; but more especially in the sparkling thoughts and pure emotions of great and holy men.

To the statement of "why I thought," it seems well

to add that the germ of the present attempt to verify miracles was of curious conception. The writer had been reflecting that, some time or other, the extraordinary idea must have sprung up amongst man's ordinary thoughts, that the mind within him—conscious also of things without him—was a witness of the Mind in nature, and yet outside of nature. That his own effort to do right, and resist wrong, had a sort of counterpart in the conflicting powers of the world, and of those outside the visible world. Light and darkness, pleasure and pain, life and death, represented the good and evil sides of existence. At first, it may be, supposing there was no Divine Revelation, he would have an intense conviction that evil could not be overcome: then experience taught him, that he was able not only to overcome some of the things that seemed against him, but actually to make them be on his side. After this the conviction arose that it was possible for some one, like but better than himself, to overcome all evil. Hence would spring the idea of a holy man, more than man, the Giver of Grace.

The thought of the thinker was at first troublous, and the old maxim—"Magna est veritas et prevalebit"—seemed to fail before the intense, subtle, insinuating, destructive power of evil. After a while, his mind became placid, in contemplation of peace by the "Giver of Peace;" and passed into quietude. Little by little everything grew up out of the indistinct grey, as of early morn, into the colour and life and movement of glorious day. All matter seemed instinct with life; every atom, of various and indescribable minuteness, vibrated with immeasurable velocity of motion; the force entering and departing gave it polarity of being. Assorting themselves, some with like, some with unlike, they grew into molecules of radiant beauty, new powers, and complex motions. Then the world sparkled with crystals, all the metals crept forth; the process being wrought as by a flash of light, yet with soft, continuous, increasing gleam; while the mystic union and interaction wrought a low sweet lisping, as were it the germ of all future speech. Nothing was still, nor silent; and the music and the motion were entrancing; but as yet, though all things lived, there was no life like that in plant, or that in living creature.

Without observation, no angel could discern the how; not by action of atom nor molecule, yet they moved; not in line or path of crystallization, but by power from nucleus which had no cell, or from fountain self-contained went forth that mysterious unfolding, the miracle of life in grass and herb and tree.

Following on, separated by intervals of degree and kind, rather than of space and time; of more lively, complex, spiral movement; and of wheel within a wheel; another life began to live: of brighter automatism, conscious sensation, and self-possession. Waters swarmed, the earth brought forth, the air teemed; and all the existence was of life by life, and kind after its kind; but eye could not see, nor ear hear, when, or how, or why, there was beginning, continuance, change, mingling, and ceasing to be. From little to great, from simple to complex, from low degree to high estate, there was mystical advance: mystical, because within the nature seeming to weave the living tissues into patterns of animals wonderful and rare, dwelt an intelligence unseen, indeed; but manifest by the very instinct of creatures which had no thought; and, yet, were guided in all necessary things as by a perfect mind. This life, with the precedent vegetable life, was in union; mutually sustentative, subordinate, yet distinct and separate; every life its own life, kind after its kind, and the vegetative apart from conscious existence.

Then came with more consciousness of growth—but it was not growth; a different separation, and a nature higher than the former degree, elevating animal from plant; an operation welding, so to speak, all nature—all life; concentrating the universe into a form of might, beauty, and intelligence, a fashion or figure of the Son of God. The frame was erect, unlike all other. The clothing was of purity—not hairy garment, nor leafy covering. The gait—divinely graceful, the symmetry—human, the face—of high-mind illumination, eyes—full of love and wonder, the brow—conscious of sovereign rule. To him was rendered a ready homage by every living thing—as if conscious of God in man; and all around was paradise.

Some noise aroused the thinker—the muser—the dreamer, whatever he was, from the pictured thought; and he saw, indeed, a tremulous vibration, and many moving gorgeous colours; but all were formed by light passing through a stained-glass window, where skilled artist had portrayed the image of Christ our Lord. Then the thinker saw a wonderful truth in fulness: all nature, all life, are of God: all men of faith live and move and have their being in Him: "ἔδωκεν αὐτοῖς ἐξουσίαν τέκνα Θεοῦ γενέσθαι τοῖς πιστεύουσιν εἰς τὸ ὄνομα αὐτοῦ" (JOHN i. 12).

It seemed that the time had come when all men should see—heart and mind being wearied with the conflict of opinion, and strife of interests, and trials of life—that they ought to trust God more; and set themselves to profit by past experience. Are we to doubt for ever, never to know? Science, alone, is not enough to content us: how unhappy is the condition of some who in science possess renown; but for whom is no glorious immortality, and whose best hope is—extinction! Culture is not enough: the Chinese, in some respects, are the most cultured people in the world; yet, life and morals are steeped in pollution. Many ancient nations possessed soundness of judgment, brightness of genius, and skill in art, unto which we moderns have not attained; yet, forsaking holiness, they perished. We need more than science, more than culture; we must listen to the voice of nature, to the Word of God. The Voice and Word are not silent: sunlight and evening shadows, promise and precept, are full of coming life and peace. By means of Faith we may have our wondering sight enraptured, and with our ears listen while Nature's music, set to words in Scripture, makes melodious the balmy air. There is in men a faculty by which they enter two regions of thought: in one, science, they are bold inquirers and sceptical reasoners; in the other they possess an inspiration and consolation, a beauty and power which renders them glad thanksgivers, obeyers, and worshippers. These men regard the outstretched sky as a canopy of love; and are sure that glories of every shape and size will illumine the Cross they bear on earth. Other men unwisely make the doubt, meant for discipline, their constant portion.

They believe not that their human form is divinely sculptured, they empty heart and mind of love and wonder, of prayer, hope of Heaven, and sense of Righteousness. They go out saddened to meet life's sorrow, weakened to earth's battle, and encounter utter defeat. Let them say henceforth—" Holy Faith has been proved again and again by the best, why doubt we with the worst? It is time that we listen to God ; and, listening, obey ; with thankfulness receive His gifts, and with righteous gladness use them ; so shall we find a preciousness everywhere. The cross that our bodies bear, and the bonds of unbelief that bound it on so tightly, shall be changed into a crown, and the bonds bind us more closely to our Lord:"—" I know the thoughts that I think toward you, saith the Lord, thoughts of peace, and not of evil, to give you an expected end" (Jer. xxix. 11).

THOUGHT I.

THE DENIAL OF MIRACLES IS UNSCIENTIFIC.

"In my opinion profound minds are the most likely to think lightly of the resources of human reason, and it is the most superficial thinker who is generally strongest in every kind of unbelief. The deep philosopher sees chains of causes and effects so wonderfully and strangely linked together, that he is usually the last person to decide upon the impossibility of any two series of events being independent of each other."

DAVY, *Salmonia.*

THE position of Spinoza, maintained by professed materialists—"Miracles are impossible, there is no transcendental beginning; for God and nature are one, from eternity to eternity"—must now, as we possess more accurate science, be abandoned.

The statement—" miracles are impossible "—cannot be maintained: it is a pure negative extending over all time, space, circumstance; and, except by an Omniscient Being, is incapable of scientific verification.

The assertion—"There is no transcendental beginning"—can only be maintained on the assumption that nature is, and ever was, in itself, organically and eternally complete: for want of completion in any of its parts would render the whole, to that extent, imperfect. That which has no beginning cannot grow in beauty and power, otherwise every act of growth would be a partial beginning. It cannot, at any time, occupy a new place;

must remain eternally the same; or move in a series of recurring cycles, in which is neither first nor last, beginning nor end. Such an assumption is incapable of verification by human reason or experience; and is, therefore, without scientific foundation. It guesses at the unknown material world by means of the known; and then denies to both that transcendental beginning without which the known, so far as physical science is concerned, could have no origination, nor development, nor change: no number of likes being able to produce an unlike. It limits possible combinations to existing mechanical arrangements, allowing neither increase nor decrease; and though these mechanical arrangements are mathematically proved to have arisen from unlike former conditions—incapable of producing them, and with which they had no physical connection, it negatives the existence of that transcendental operation apart from which could be no beginning such as our cosmogony reveals.

The two rash negatives are followed by a bold positive—"God and nature are one from eternity to eternity." This positive is essentially weak on the negative side; for that God was never a separate Existence, nor apart from nature; and does not, never did, and never can exceed nature; is utterly incapable of proof. The affirmative side is not more accurate: for to say that our conception and knowledge of God and nature are so all-containing and assured that nothing in heaven or earth escapes us; and that everything in the past, the present, the future, may be thus comprehensively formulated—"God is *natura naturans*, and nature is *natura naturata*;" God was never without the world, and the world is God Himself, shocks our common sense.

In contrast with such boastful statements concerning God and the world, and in proof that even a small part of that world cannot be fully searched out, remember that no one can tell the secret of atomic obedience in the familiar changes from ice to steam; nor tell the acting law of the pressures and resistances which a flying bird encounters, all around, from the atmosphere; nor are the forces at work in our finger-nail, or in our hairs, or in the hair of a nettle, scientifically understood. Think of the entomologist, Pierre Lyonnet, devoting many years to the study of one insect, *Phalæna cossus*, a caterpillar which infects the willow-tree. The book describing and figuring it is a quarto volume of more than six hundred pages, adorned with eighteen plates. The number of muscles alone, all described and figured, is four thousand and forty-one. The labour, nevertheless, did not acquire all the knowledge; nor does the book narrate all that is to be narrated; nor do the plates, nor the muscles described and figured, reveal more than a small part of the mystery and the wonder contained in that one insect.

Bearing in mind a further fact—that every event, even the most trifling, is so complicate and multiform in its antecedents, that we have given up our quest as to the cause of anything, we repudiate the following statement as inaccurate and presumptuous—" Miracles, or the intervention of the Deity in human affairs, are, to the scientific thinker, *a priori*, so improbable, that no amount of testimony suffices to make him entertain the hypothesis for an instant." This assertion exceeds all

The Denial of Miracles is Unscientific. 13

that science can know or affirm ; in fact is utterly unscientific, and can never be accepted by an accurate, comprehensive, disciplined intellect. Indeed, it is utterly impossible to give an exhaustive scientific statement of the continuous behaviour of the acting energies of any three masses, or force points, in any cubical quarter-inch of force-locus, animate or inanimate, in air, or earth, or sea, for one minute preceding or following any moment that men may select. The man of science, however, can clearly show that the present state of things is derivative—is not what it originally was : he can prove that the whole pomp of stars and all the variety of life have been originated. The fact becomes truly self-evident to the thinker : for the universe now existing is proved, on mechanical principles, to have had a beginning in a state of things where and when the laws known to us were not in being ; nor could they have been originated therein except by energy from without. Professor P. G. Tait states ("Recent Advances in Physical Science," p. 26)—" all portions of our science, and especially that beautiful one the Dissipation of Energy, points unanimously to a beginning, to a state of things incapable of being derived by present laws (of tangible matter and its energy) from any conceivable previous arrangement." Thus, we have not only established our argument—" the denial of miracles is unscientific "—but have shown that our present science affirms the greatest of all miracles—a Beginning, a Creation.

THOUGHT II.

NATURALISM AND SUPERNATURALISM.

"Our notions of what is natural will be enlarged in proportion to our greater knowledge of the works of God and the dispensations of His Providence."—BISHOP BUTLER.

NATURALISM—as opposed to Supernaturalism, maintaining that the system of laws of matter, of space, of energy, which we are conscious of in nature, either had no beginning, or began and exists by its own originative and continuative power; and contains within its own limits and variations the whole universe, actual and possible, finally and eternally fixed—is convicted of inadequacy. It applies the limited measure of human intellect, and the inaccuracy of human knowledge, to that infinitude which can neither be measured, nor fully known. It says—"There was nothing before matter, there is no existence apart from it, there will be nothing after it. Matter, driven by force within space, is the whole of nature: all within is mechanism, but there is no mechanic; and outside of it is no being—no life." Such a theory narrows the universe into a mechanical system, and makes human experience and conception a limit of possibility. Those who maintain it cannot draw, even as to objects of appreciable magnitude, much less in the illimitable vast of the indescribably minute, an accurate line between the conscious and the unconscious—those two departments into which they divide the cosmos; nor can they prove that the latter exists; nor are they able to determine whether the minimum force-locus is a solid atom, or a point without parts— that is, a finite minimum having parts, or a point having position and no parts. It is really too bad that necessarians, positivists, materialists, who cannot write down with proof the scientific expression of any three different laws continuously at work from point to point, from moment to moment, in the universe, should disgust us with their sickening pretences to universality of knowledge. We will not say with Thomas Penyngton Kirkman that their variety of expressions and decorations of sophisms move in "a donkey's circle;" but we adopt his words as to the theories—"They are merely the rags that hang, not sweetly, on the shivering flanks of Ignorance."

Laying aside the wrong view, take the right view of Naturalism. Properly, "the only distinct meaning of the word natural is stated, fixed, settled." We may argue, in fashion of Butler's "Analogy," that "what is natural as much requires and presupposes an intelligent Mind to render it so—that is to effect it continually or at stated times—as what is supernatural or miraculous does to effect it for once." A miracle, then, is unusual Divine action; natural law is habitual Divine action. In a world containing creatures that are really free, both kinds of action are essential; otherwise, freedom is not freedom. The natural is, indeed, a continual miracle, but being prolonged hides its supernaturalism from the common observer. It represents the truth—God is so wise that He can make all things; and, much wiser than that, He enables all things to make themselves.

Supernaturalism—as opposed to Atheistic Naturalism, maintains that even the atoms march in tune—as if the music had been set; and that the commonest substances in nature, moving to the music of law, are a miracle of beauty by some Wonder Worker. Supernaturalism maintains that our experience is continually enlarging; that we are for ever discovering within ourselves and without ourselves new potencies, new laws, new operations, new combinations; that the preceding stages of human life were preparations for later developments; and that man being greatly in correlation with nature, it follows that nature, of which he forms part, is likewise a series of changes which are teleological developments of former potencies.

In other words—Nature, on the objective side of existence, shows that the meanest of living things share our pedigree, are "all souls of fire and children of the sun." Nature, on the inner or subjective side, shows that even the solid matter of our woods, our rocks, and our own organisms, was disguised in semi-transparent gas, with atoms and molecules attracting and repelling: so that all forms, inorganic and organic, are an expression of marvellous, ethereal, complicate, molecular action and interaction. These objective and subjective sides of existence are as the concave and convex lenses, used in our process of microscopic and telescopic investigation, whereby we discover that things are not without wonder and mystery; not in inner form as they outwardly seem, nor were formerly as they now are, nor are as they will be.

Observe those fern-like forms which, on a frosty morning, overspread your window-panes. By breathing on one of the panes, dissolve the solid crystalline film to a liquid condition, then watch:—so soon as you cease breathing, the film—by action of its own forces—seems to be alive (a common magnifying glass shows it very beautifully), lines of motion radiate, molecule closes with molecule, until the whole film passes from the liquid state to crystalline repose.

These straight lines, curves, definite arrangements of particles, by polar and other forces, in exquisite structure, cannot be explained as caused by the separate independent attraction and repulsion of self-positing molecules : for structural, that is complex architectural and organic action, requires other more and higher powers than the atomic and molecular. The difference and nature are wide apart as the structure of a stone and the construction of a palace ; as fire-mist of the sky and finished worlds. This fact is overlooked by professors of naturalism, and it renders their theory incompetent to explain the universe as an organic whole. Atoms and molecules being satisfied by mutual embrace, an energy infinitely more comprehensive than that of these numerals builds them up into the various wonderful equations and endless variety of worlds.

We carry back our scientific imagination to the first beginning of things. We see molecules assuming visible form through aggregation of invisible atoms by means of polar and other forces. There is passage from the gaseous to the fluid, from the fluid to the solid, and cloud-masses are formed into suns, planets, satellites, comets. Vegetable organisms are built up through the reduction of chemical compounds, and rounded off by hardly discernible shades of increasing vitality. Animal life exists by more or less complicate reversals of reduction; and, in ascending scales, perfected in the human organism. The process is not by atomic energy, but by a directing, distributive, cumulating, constructive principle essentially apart from the molecules themselves, but acting in and by them : for a process almost the same, and with materials well-nigh identical, weaves the texture of a frog, and organizes man.

From the above, it is evident that nature is not without transcendental beginning; that, indeed, there are many new and continual transcendent beginnings. Transcendent because the varieties and ascending stages of existence could not possibly be wrought by one process of mechanism, and with one kind of material; but are the product of varying and greater energies continually flowing in to control and elevate lower forms and powers, to renew and enlarge activities, to mould into higher organic completeness. Far from nature being the same through all eternity, there is a display of endless variety, a passing through new stages, an assuming of new forms, acquisition of new powers, and adornment with new beauties. Nature awakes from the equilibrium of repose to the conflict of mechanical forces, thence to sensitive life, thence to intellectual activities, thence to the moral emotions of righteousness. Nature may be termed the law of God's ever-working will. It is so perfect in its provisions for every possible event or combination of events, that it requires no new or additional legislation, no acts to repeal, no acts to amend. Seeing, however, when our souls are full of awe before this majesty that we, so far as we are free, can and do distort law; that we are conscious of moral evil which cannot be attributed to the All-Good; we recognize an advance, or remedial process, which seems more directly in connection with the Power working for righteousness:

> "From seeming evil still educing good,
> And better thence again, and better still,
> In infinite progression."

The advance—whether physical or moral, by energies from within nature, or by energies from without nature—is not so much by the past containing the future, but rather by the future retaining and exalting the past; and the ascent warrants our intellectual and emotional conviction that, in due time, the universe will represent, as in a glass, free from obliquity, speck, and discolouring, the perfected work of One—

> "Whose voice is on the rolling air;
> We hear Him where the waters run;
> He standeth in the rising sun,
> And in the setting He is fair."

Science does not find that investigation renders the world less wonderful, all things mechanical, and men brutal. Gaining a firmer, fuller grasp of truth, she passes on the lamp of knowledge from generation to generation for illumination of the world, as a kingdom built up *in gloriam fidei in gloriam Dei*. The strange story of a Progressing Kingdom, which all accept, the Secularist believing in man, and the Christian believing in God, testifies to something more than a blind whirlpool or eddy of fate. The ascent from slime and ooze not being by innumerable stages of mechanical ascent, not by casual improvement of brutes; but by entrance of creative, quickening, mental and moral influences; joint operations of will and might; the kingdom and progress being placed above doubt by their very nature and purity: for how could Folly fabricate a narrative or process of Wisdom; when and how was it possible in a world which had no trace, nor sign, nor thought, nor consciousness of God, to fable of His Existence, Righteousness, and of Judgment to Come?

Surely, those who go about in miscalculating unbelief, teaching a naturalness which is unnatural, are in great ignorance, and much in want of better employment. Their true vocation in the world is to live, and to teach, a nobler life than that.

THOUGHT III.

INNER IMPULSE TO THE MIRACULOUS.

> ". . . . From higher to higher:
> As mounts the heavenward altar-fire."

OH! the peace and joy of having attained some blessed height, in surety of faith, whence to look undismayed on all that history, that criticism, that science may discover. We may attain that height; possess faith, unshaken by earth's convulsions; faith, enduring to life's end; faith —loving, trusting, reverencing—built on the knowledge that the clusters of imagination in Homer, Dante, Milton, Shakespeare; the light of reason in Socrates, Plato, Bacon, Newton; the Divinity in Moses, Isaiah, Daniel; were regenerating energies for the world.

We ascend the height by means of facts which are acknowledged even by unbelieving men.

Unbelievers are well aware, if acquainted with modern science, that natural phenomena or material existences are the raiment or visible appearance of some inner invisible Power. Scientific men are almost unanimous that matter is not "force," but "the condition of force." Æther is scientifically defined as an assemblage of vibrations. Light comes by the marvellous vibrations of æther, and sound propagates itself by means of atmospheric undulations. For matter to attract and light to shine without the medium of æther, and sound to be heard apart from undulations of the air, would be a miracle; and miracles are not allowed by the materialist. Notwithstanding, the intellect, the inner spirit feels, sees, and hears light and sound, without intervention of objective reality; and these facts are somewhat akin to the miraculous.

For example—The doctrines, the mysteries, the hopes, mental and emotional powers dealt with in Sacred Literature, are regarded by profane persons not as fictions or lies, but as destitute of any substantial or objective reality. The fact is utterly ignored, that our mental and emotional consciousness is the measure and gauge of even material being—

> "Ours is the cloth, the pencil, and the paint,
> Which nature's admirable picture draws;
> And beautifies creation's ample dome.
> Like Milton's Eve, when gazing on the lake,
> Man makes the matchless image man admires."
>
> *Night Thoughts.*

The fact is also forgotten, that it is equally impossible for the uncaused to exist in either. Volition, conviction, faith, uncaused—if they rest not on some ultimate reality—are an effect without cause; which is absurd or a miracle. Ascending the Mount of Transfiguration, it is allowed that a pure glow of inner splendour lighted up the Saviour's mind to a consciousness of Divine Glory, and of the prophets' spiritual presence. It is confessed that our Lord, Peter, James, and John, looking within themselves, might find the inward glow of Heavenly radiance. That radiance might be automatic, or by a spontaneity quickened by great expectations in the Master and in the men; but could not, so we are assured, possess objective reality.

Accordingly, we possess an inner impulse to faith in, and a conscious realization of, the miraculous which is wholly unaccountable: for there is not, and never was, fairly stating the Materialist's argument, any actual miracle or Divine manifestation to excite that impulse and consciousness. Here is a marvel indeed: for human intelligence and emotion can no more create the existing universal belief in, and consciousness of, Divinity and of Divine Action, than it can evoke the visible material phenomena as counterpart. Manifestly, our opponents' argument goes on unequal feet: there cannot be mental miracles, if physical marvels are impossible; our nature does not contradict itself; and as, indeed, no man is able precisely to fix the separating barriers between objectiveness and subjectiveness, between substance and intelligence, least of all Materialists, we safely regard the inner universal impulse to the marvellous as an inwrought proof of miracles.

Alike in the external and internal worlds, we find ourselves amidst perpetual changes, of which we see neither beginning nor end. If we entertain the hypothesis that all matter existed once in a diffused form, we find it utterly impossible to conceive how this came to be so. When speculating on the future, a grand succession of phenomena is ever unfolding before us. Striving to find the essential nature of things we are utterly at fault; nor can we, as to our own consciousness, remember when it began; or examine our consciousness that at any present moment exists; for only that already past, never one which is passing, can become the object of thought. We are brought, in every direction, face to face with the unknowable. An impenetrable mystery underlies all things. We find, notwithstanding, that our conscience makes a law for us, and that all promulgated laws are the work of individual consciences—a latent work lasting sometimes through many centuries. Law implies responsibility, and ten thousand million convincing voices, within and without, in this daily course of life and sin and mercy assert that we are responsible to the living God, a Ruler who knows that He is ruling, a Worker who knows that He is working, a Giver and Lover who knows that He is giving and loving. The ground of it all being an inner impulse t the miraculous.

THOUGHT IV.

WORLD WITHIN THE WORLD.

"Only in Reality lies the essence and foundation of all that was ever fabled, visioned, sung, spoken, or babbled by the human species; and the actual Life of Man includes in it all Revelations, true and false, that have been, are, or are to be."—THOMAS CARLYLE.

NOT only the conduct, but the character of individuals and nations, depends on their belief and will.

Belief and will do not originate nor expand of themselves in the spirit. They are formed by the operation of our consciousness on the experience of life. Belief in the wonderful, the miraculous, is world-wide. The most powerful mover of the will; that which has played the greatest part in the history of the Earth; that which animates to marvellous exertions, and furnishes brightest hopes and direst fears to heart and mind; is our sense of the Supernatural.

How belief can be excited, the will put in action, and moral obligations established, so that physical acts shall result from mental determination; apart from actual material occurrences, seen marvels, and known deliverances, is a mystery. If there is no God, and men invented Him; then, men are able to fashion in their own minds a more wonderful Being and Existence than the universe either represents or contains—this, in itself, partakes of the miraculous. If there are no miracles, men have pictured to themselves operations the like of which cannot be found in Heaven or Earth— this, in itself, is supernatural. The world within is proved to be more marvellous than the world without. The invention of universal conviction as to marvels, and of all-pervading consciousness as to God, conviction and consciousness resulting from no ultimate cause, without even an antecedent, are miracles.

We will now apply the thought.

If all causes and antecedents are material; if all being and existence are comprised in matter, force, space; how can the inner character and outer conduct of Hebrews and Christians be explained apart from those marvels on which their faith and history immovably rest? He who says — "Historical monuments, national institutions, public ceremonies, grandest lives, heroic achievements, sublimest deaths, events of world-wide interest, transactions so majestic that all others are small in comparison; are based on delusive notions; are not realized truth, but flights of falsest fancy; and erections on groundless superstitions;" expects every man to be counted a liar, and himself alone as true. Even so, how will this miracle of a man account for these notions, flights, superstitions, seeing that there is not even the shadow of a shade of reality in any of them; and in us no power of creating absolute impossibilities? We cannot move a limb without some substratum of fact; how, then, has the whole world been moved to faith in miracles without the grain of mustard-seed for reality? There must be a world within the world.

That, however, does not conform to the materialistic

statement—"The external world is the only reality;" but every one not a Materialist, capable of accurate scientific thought, has been fully persuaded that there is an inner world. Every one: for the bonds of organic union, personality, and identity, which make man to be man, are not wholly physical as to their incircling: we possess states of consciousness and continually perform mental acts which testify of things immaterial—things utterly transcending and contrary to all that is possible in physics.

For example: The mind is at times apart from the body—so far as consciousness goes: we possess permanent mental and emotional states concerning things which, materially, are impossible; and seem to have means of knowledge transcending those called natural. All that we know has two faces: Mind, a floating succession of ideas; Matter, a floating consciousness of phenomena. The passage from one to the other we cannot understand; and transfer from the homogeneous to the heterogeneous seems of a transcendental character; even as, to our present knowledge, are the media influencing the translation of heat, light, electricity, magnetism, gravity.

The fact may be put into physiological form:—The development of the frontal lobes of the brain is greatest in those men who possess the highest intellectual powers. "Electrical irritation of the antero-frontal lobes causes no motor manifestations," says Dr. Ferrier ("Functions of the Brain," p. 287). It follows, "that though not motor, they are inhibitory motor, and expend their energy in inducing internal changes in the centres of actual motor execution." Consequently, the keys on which the anthem of high intelligence and emotion is played are the frontal portion of the brain; and the anthem is played—not by electrical, or physical, that is mechanical, irritation, but by an invisible musician—let us say—"the spirit of life."

We may carry this a little further. Take a few words of the philosopher, Ueberweg—"What occurs in the brain, would, in my opinion, not be possible, if the process, which here appears in its greatest concentration, did not obtain generally, only in a vastly diminished degree." That is—there is a kind of life even in particles that are not organized. The flesh, which we eat, is not wholly dead; the flour, which we bake, contains though weak and pale that which concentrated in the brain manifests highest living and intellectual powers. There may be minima of life going far below all that we possess any knowledge of, and maxima extending far beyond our every thought. Nevertheless, we cannot regard the particles of water, of albumen, of carbon, as possessing any sense or consciousness of life; they neither think, nor feel; all matter is not two-sided in the sense that conscious living matter is. Truly, the world within the world is full and rich; nor is it any paradox to assert—in the profundity are depths transcending all material limits. A mystery—a miracle lies at the foundation of all matter, moves in everything that lives, and animates all intelligence.

Suppose we say—"Matter is eternal;" that seems a less reasonable begging of the question than to say—"God is Eternal." Less reasonable, we say: for, behold a greater miracle! you must give to matter the attributes of mind—to possess that and life in itself; so, *de facto*, making it god, though you say, "there is no God." Hence, he who postulates the eternity of matter, rather than the eternity of God; does thereby postulate Divine Existence also—in degraded form—a Mind materially imprisoned.

"If matter is not eternal, its first emergence into being is a miracle beside which all others sink into absolute insignificance;" but we are told, as if we did not know it—"That is unthinkable." Will they tell us in what way the eternity of matter is more thinkable than the creation of matter? Will any Materialist think out for us, and make it plain, that the sudden apocalypse of a material world out of blank nonentity is more unthinkable than the eternal existence of many or innumerable worlds? Until he has performed the task, suppose that we think a little for ourselves. It does not seem so difficult, after all, to think in a serviceable sort of way: that God so made all things out of nothing; that by a beginning, very long ago, there was a chaos in which all things were "without form and void." Then there was that wonderful advance into light, life, and replenishing; so beautifully given in the grand old Book, that even the less-gifted men—those incapable of the faith that sublimes—can regard it as a true poetic rendering of the scientific doctrine of slow evolution.

It is not, however, necessary that we accept the doctrine of evolution—not even to the extent that science affirms—our science is not final. We believe that the whole process is far more wonderful than the wisest can conceive. When fully known, in the days of our enlargement, the knowledge now possessed will seem as the groping of children in the dark. Let us, meanwhile, be thankful for what we know. The scientific view as far exceeds the common view, as that surpasses the fetichism of a savage; and beyond the horizon is that unseen—is that inexplicable—which comes near to our consciousness, and our spirit sees and hears mysterious sights and sounds. Alas! all too soon withdrawn: and, yet, they make us happy. Nor is there any man, of high style and ripened spirit, without that God-consciousness of world within the world by which he has foretaste of things to come.

THOUGHT V.

HIDDEN THINGS.

"'What is it thou knowest, sweet voice?' I cried,
'A hidden hope,' the voice replied."
The Two Voices—TENNYSON.

WE stand in the lapse of time—eternity behind, eternity before—we are ignorant of actual facts, yet cannot lay down any limit to possible knowledge. We are borne along by an irresistible and inexplicable tide of force: for between the force of gravitation and force of thought what an interval! and who shall explain it? Nor is that all—"Le temps, la matière, et l'espace, ne sont peut-être qu'un point"—time, matter, space, are perhaps but a point; nevertheless, the lordliest phantasmagory which we name Being is around us, and under us, in the wonderful earth. Overhead, the infinite height with greater and lesser lights, bright-rolling, silent-beaming, hurled forth by the Hand of Might; as if the small strophe of every human life, having such embellishment, was joined with the occasional verse of other earthly existence, into some grand anthem; to be sung at last in praise of Supernal Power.

Plato, in his "Phædon" (Jowett's Translation, vol. i. pp. 465, 466), relates a saying of Socrates concerning that most mysterious and hidden of things, the spirit of man—"You may bury me if you can catch me!" Then he added with a smile of thought and tenderness—"Do not call this poor body Socrates. When I have drunk the poison, I shall leave you and go to the joys of the blessed. I would not have you sorrow at my hard lot, or say at the interment, 'Thus we lay out Socrates,' or 'Thus we follow him to the grave, or bury him.' Be of good cheer; say that you are burning my body only." Heroic human strophes of this kind are few. You cannot exact them from inferior men; and yet, a certain perennial spirit looks through the thinking of all who are of highest order, enabling them to see the gleaming rainbow of creation brightening in the light of God; while others seem conscious only of everlasting storm, which no one governs, wild, roaring, rushing torrent-wise, thundering down, and then falling silent —of oblivion swallowed.

He who maintains that marvels thus found in the thin rind of the Conscious, and other marvels in that fathomless domain the Unconscious, have no meaning; that every worm, toiling, spins its own cocoon; but everything is without knitted purport, and points to no reality; must really stand without the Sanctuary of Man's Soul, and imagine that where his hand ceases to grope the world ends. He must be deaf to the Sacred Melody, heavenly toned, "as from some blissful neighbourhood," wherein are harmony and meaning for ever. He can only just attain to that poorest of all philosophy, the Mechanical, which has no room for Divinity; and can do no more than doubt concerning that moral stage which is proof of man's immortal being. He tells us—"Nature whirls round in endless Mahlstroms, both creating and swallowing itself." Then he says—"We cannot picture out and arrange in our diagram of worlds, nor include within our philosophy, the Highest Infinite." This we are told as if we knew it not, and he talks doubtfully concerning proof of God, of a probable God, of no God ; as if the finding and comprehending of that All-glorious One, apart from Revelation, would not be indeed a miracle.

Now, though by our own unaided searching we cannot perfectly find out God, every person capable of reasoning on these subjects is aware that, by help of symbols, defined as unknown principles, we can and do reason, to a certain extent, as correctly as were we actually masters of those principles. For example: A is the universe ; P is the principle of order contained in the universe ; N is a competent intelligence, with power of application and illustration, able to deduce any known definite fact (Q) as the logical consequence flowing out of the principle (P). The theorem can be varied, and P be taken as the principle of order transcending, or uncontained in, the universe ; and so on. The theorem may be tested in this way : P is the principle of order in (or if you will, transcending) A, the universe ; then B is the beauty, C is the consciousness, D is the danger, and so on with any fact ; then N is able to deduce this B, or C, or D, as a part of the principle (P) in or transcending A, the universe. We will now, seeing that by means of the known we may reason in some measure correctly concerning the unknown, investigate a few strange realities.

The investigator, causing the mystic play of thoughts to assume definite form, passes to the study of minute organisms. Some of these are bodies 80,000th or 120,000th of an inch in diameter; or, say, we measure them in terms of the lengths of the luminiferous waves; thus possibilities which seemed romantic enter the region of fact. There are beings of minuteness which, though discoverable by science, is inconceivable by the mind. Again—we find that the infinitesimal ripples of a vibrating plate will actually turn sound into electricity, and electricity into sound; and that there is in nature a continual becoming of things into that which they are not; and so far from there being any dead or lifeless form of continuity, a voltaic discharge, even when apparently continuous, is a succession of intermediencies at exceedingly short intervals. Further—we see in the same day brutes on the summit of a mountain, and men at the foot, with regard to whom the quadruped seems to have the superiority in all that we desire should live. We find animals tapering down by wholly inappreciable gradations to the lowest organisms, and thence to inorganic elements. We also find an ascent from lower grades to higher states, until some of the noblest animals attain, if not possession, proximity to that moral condition which constitutes man an immortal being.

As to the hidden principles at work in all these marvels, there are various ways of reading the mystical language, according to the proportion of scientific and Scriptural culture. To some men, life—all life, is a Divine matter: to others—as if it grew by chance or fate, and presents no riddle; and they ask not Whence, nor Why, nor Whither, is it tending? We may pass from individuals to nations. The Greeks were in earnest, and brought forth from their gaze of nature a radiant smiling fleshly grace of Life; so that it proceeded in figures of immortal beauty from the chisel of ancient sculptors. One class of Oriental mind, specially that of the Magi, found semi-sensual grandeurs and splendours in Life; and, at times, Nature appeared in more terrible form, as glowing fire on back-ground of infinite darkness. Another and better class of Orientalism, read the language of Life and Nature closely, and in earnest, as something very Sacred—wholly Divine, Heaven-written. We moderns, endeavouring to unite science and sacred emotion in one and the same intellect, give accuracy to the former and to the latter reasonableness. The process is somewhat as follows. Naturally, the Earth is mother, and the Sun is father of all living. From the ground, unorganized, proceeded those germs which, quickened by heat and light, advanced to primal life. This life flowed in two streams: the one a river of life for all vegetation, the other a stream of animal existence. All germs, so far as we know at present, were and are essentially the same; yet contain within the sameness elements of marvellous diversity. We apportion that wonderful development the animal kingdom into these realms: Protozoa, Cœlenterata, Annuloida, Annulosa, Mollusca, and Vertebrata. Evolution, so far as verified, traces all this varied life from one and the same structureless life-matter. The growth is always chiefest along lines in the direction of least resistance, or in obedience to impulse of most active vital energy. The progress may be rectilinear, or diagonal, or curved, or circular, or spiral, or in any other form, indeed the sub-kingdoms exhibit every conceivable mode of advance. Another series of facts is observed in connection with the process of evolution—the accomplishment of great changes, and advance, or retrogression, with least possible expenditure of time. This accounts for the leaps by which several stages of the ordinary process are not unfrequently jumped over, and explains the absence of intermediary forms.

We will now advance from these hidden things of matter and of time to that which is more recondite—the mind. To see and to hear with the spirit those infinitesimal creatures measured by lengths of luminiferous waves, and to comprehend the continual becoming of things into that which they are not, require a sense over and above the ordinary five—a sixth sense—insight; in like manner to discern everywhere and in everything the All-knowing, the All-working, in whom all things move and have their being, is to possess that Spirit which becomes a Divine Magnetism, drawing a man Heaven-ward, so that he consciously lays hold of eternal life.

Thus to think, is not that bringing together of the true and the false out of which men manufacture the plausible. The most cautious mathematicians admit into their calculations quantities which, by their own showing, are imaginary or impossible; and have to form new algebras which possess no counterpart in reality, yet are means of arrival not only at possibles but actuals. The most clear-headed men are engaged in problems like the following:—Measure a line in one direction, or in the opposite; reckon time forward or backward; perform an operation, or reverse it; do it, or undo it. If, having once reversed one of these processes, we reverse it a second time, we shall find that we come back to the original direction of measurement, or of reckoning, or of original operation. Suppose now that, at some stage of a calculation, our formula indicates an alteration such that, if the alteration be repeated, a condition of things not the same as, but the reverse of, the original will be produced; or suppose that time is to be reckoned some way different from future and past, but still in a way having some definite algebraical connection with time that is gone and with time to come. It is clear that actual experience affords no process to which such measurements of space and time respond: nevertheless, we attain abstract definite points of issue concerning space and infinitude, time and eternity; and ought to give a rational account of the puzzle.

It partially removes the difficulty if we say—"The formulæ are more comprehensive than their assigned signification; but, on a more enlarged basis, the formulæ may be capable of interpretation. The difficulties, indeed, indicate that there must be some more comprehensive statement of the problem including cases impossible in the more limited."

These imaginaries, called up by legitimate processes of science, actually conduct to practical conclusions. Take, for example, Professor James Thompson's machine, which, by friction of a disc, a cylinder, and a ball, effects a variety of complicate calculations, and enables an unskilled hand to do the work of ten arithmeticians. No machinery, however, can effect the work of a living organism, which instantaneously converts dead matter into living substance, giving it a nucleus, and within that a nucleolus. From these little wells, or founts of life—which may exist and work, strange to say, without cell-wall or centre, in less than every portion of five-hundredth part of an inch in our body—proceed the threads of nerves, of arteries, of muscle, of bone, and all the mechanism of our system. The same causes not producing the same results, the difference in results being indeed measureless; yet, the bioplasm always the same, so far as we know, in every tissue. Not only does the mystic play weave fibre round fibre spirally, the whole complexity of tissue is woven together into a conscious responsible being able to know God, to glorify God, and enjoy Him for ever.

Our process of thought proves that the definiteness of mathematics becomes fictitious, if all its conclusions are pressed as necessarily final, and at the cost of spiritual meaning. Beyond the range of subject matters, not perfectly uniform, strict use of the science will hinder—not help thought. The mechanical system may possibly be a sort of ballast to our aspirations concerning purity, spiritual life, and Divine Life, but must not be allowed to weaken those receptive and constructive faculties of our consciousness by means of which we find or create objective reality in many things that are incapable of physical embodiment. We may, so to speak, change our magnet, and pass through various bodily mental and emotional states; change water to gases, and gases to water; unfold and re-fold the textures of organisms again and again; but once loose the living strands of existence, and no human skill is able to join them again together. By means of hidden powers the lion and the swallow, the plant and man, are woven by the loom of nature into their manifold and multiform web of life. Marvellously intricate processes go forward in apparently structureless matter. Things are done for which neither means nor causes are seen in operation. Matter and its forces alike come from the unseen, as were they a birth from the preceding invisible. There are influences which we cannot fathom, nor mete; but their operations—however inscrutable, and, as we have seen, effected without apparent means, therefore, of miraculous aspect—obtain a large and important place among the natural facts of our existence.

THOUGHT VI.

ARE MIRACLES IMPROBABLE?

> "Carve out
> Free space for every human doubt,
> That the whole mind may orb about."
>
> *The Two Voices.*

MIRACLES are asserted to be so improbable, that "no amount of testimony suffices to make a scientific thinker entertain, for a moment, any idea of their reality."

The assertion must be met with plain speaking and utter denial—it is untrue. Scientific thinkers, the greatest and furthest sighted of men, the most experienced and prudent persons in the world, whether of past or present time, have received and do receive miracles as one of the modes in which God reveals Himself to men.

The miracles of Holy Scripture are not connected with silly credulous prattle, but associated with words of imperishable wisdom; are not united to low and ignorant superstition, but to highest moral culture, and to those exalted views of life which honour and bless human existence. They are parts of the experience and doings of men whose sagacity and experience placed them above deception; whose purity and grandeur rendered them incapable of deceit. Miracles—as revealing and confirming truths which could only be miraculously known and affirmed; as acts—linked with words of knowledge that instruct and win dominion over profoundest minds; as doings of God, of angels, of Christ, received by purest hearts — approved by strongest minds—producing the most sacred and useful lives—have that testimony which renders it impossible, even to the miraculous itself, that they should not have been performed.

Seeing that all testimony must be repudiated, if this evidence is refused; the wisest men charged with folly, if these are to be accounted silly; the most stupendous and sacred acts in the world rendered contemptible, if these are to be deemed a lie; all religion declared false, if Christianity is to be accounted a myth; all our faith, all our hope, all our future, the knowledge of God, the fact of Judgment to Come, and the responsibility of man to Deity, be scattered to the winds, if miracles are unworthy of credit; we do well to inquire concerning the asserted improbability.

It is a physical improbability. It is a departure from the usual course of things—a deviation from common law. Our Lord's walking on the sea, and His raising of Lazarus, were miracles. The common experience of men is that the dead do not live again, and that he who takes a watery path will sink like Peter. No living man would be credited if he said—" I have walked on the deep from Dover to Calais." Were any one raised from the dead, in the sight of many witnesses, who, not seeing, would believe? The true idea, then, of a miracle, is that of an effect in nature, which, at present, can only be accounted for as the result of an original or direct movement from the Divine Centre.

Are direct movements from the Divine Centre so improbable as to render faith in their occurrence impossible? Is the law—that we know, and the course of it—as to our experience, so fixed and all-embracing that there could not be, and never has been, greater liberty and enlargement? Are we to jump at the unknown and say—"It is the double of that with which we are acquainted?" Certainly not. Will Materialists fully explain any one act, any one event, any one existence, as independent of, or apart from, that Inscrutable Energy of which the whole universe is a manifestation? They cannot explain. Everything we know, whether in nature or history, inorganic or organic, though the way was prepared for it, and its appearance was conditioned by existing forces, had origin, so science asserts, in a condition anterior to all present existence; and in state and place where and when the forces now in operation were non-existent. When, as Materialists cannot separate any phenomenon from the universal Energy; and as inquiry concerning antecedents leads very quickly to the transcendental, bringing the inquirer face to face with the incomprehensible and inexplicable; it follows that everything of which we are conscious is found to pass beyond common law and experience; and to be, so far as we are able to judge, a result of action from the great Centre—to be, in fact, a miracle.

Not only the origin of things, their course also soon passes beyond the limits of our knowledge. Nor only so, every stage in the process of advance, of evolution, of creation, is a mystery, and every step in departure is a marvel. There is no transition from the inorganic to the organic, and no passage from being to not being, that our science so formulates as to afford us real cognition. It is not possible, by any mere mechanical process of self-development, to bring out of atoms or organisms anything not potentially in them. Every epoch in life, in the history of the world, specially those epochs realizing a new and essentially higher form of existence, of power, of beauty, of freedom, must and do find their only sufficient cause in the Omnipotent Energy.

We will now somewhat change the form of our thought.

The constitution of existing nature is an example of continual advances; advances previously altogether unimaginable. Man is a miracle to the beast, the beast is a miracle to the plant, the plant is a miracle to the stone; and you may take, if you please, the intervening grades as naturalization of the miracles. First came energies, we do not now concern ourselves with the origin of matter, regulating inorganic matter— then those of vegetation, afterwards those of animal life, culminating in marvellous human powers. Could a thinking mineral account for the laws of vegetable growth by a new kind of accretion? Would a vegetable, in one of its sports, devise a power of animal life? and a ruminating animal aspire to manhood and attain it?

The progression is conceivable as we look back; it was an absolute mystery and inconceivable while yet future. Those who believe that the advance was so gradual, even imperceptible, that there never was any real advance, nor any miracle, all being an easy onward flow, make miracles beautifully easy, and, no doubt, can construct a plane to ascend so gradually and exquisitely that water may be coaxed to run up hill. Other people will maintain that miracles are not improbable—are not unusual—the whole basis of things is miraculous; nature is one splendid miracle.

An acute sceptical mind may object—that if we define miracle in one way, even Hume will admit miracle; if in another way, to cover special and unusual operations, many will deny. We answer—our process of thought proves that Nature is a splendid and continual miracle: to quibble about smaller matters is to "strain at a gnat and swallow a camel." This, however, will be dealt with in another place.

We take a further thought:—

Within a definite time, say ten or twelve millions of years ago, our earth was uninhabitable. Then our Homers and Shakespeares, Moses and Isaiah, Newton and Pascal, were not. Think of the upward progress through myriads of centuries; then carry thought to the time, in part calculable, when the habitable globe shall drag down and destroy humanity in its own extinction; when Dante and Milton, Patriarchs and Saints, the miseries and aspirations of mankind, so far as they are then of the earth, shall be thrust again into darkness and death. Is it probable that we are thus played with by chance, or that evil fate destroys us, as a wicked child plays with a drowning animal? Has the struggle been without a Will? Is the intelligence without any Heart of Reason, or the upward progress without Direction? If so, what is all our science worth? If we are at the end, and not in the first part of our Play, what avail the good longing for more good, truth for more truth, and life for more life? Shall we accept this despairing creed—irrational as hopeless? Nay. Our physical science shall perform her part in the world's development—perform it humbly; remembering that her province is but an infinitesimal portion of the vast sphere of knowledge, and that she can but touch the hem of the garment of Majesty. Our body with its sensations, our mind with its science, our spirit with its sacred emotions, are keys that unlock and open the doors of many chambers of mysteries in our Father's House. We, entering these chambers, know that there are miracles in a tree, a stone, a withered leaf, in the broad ocean and azure heaven; but more specially in those blessed minds who consciously hold communion with the Eternal.

> "Such minds are truly from the Deity,
> For they are Powers; and hence the highest bliss
> That men can know is theirs; the consciousness
> Of whom they are, habitually infused
> Through every image and through every thought."

THOUGHT VII.

IS BELIEF IN MIRACLES UNREASONABLE?

> "Ex atrâ veniunt clarissima fulgura nube,
> Aurum de rutilo clarius igne micat."

> "A number of propositions, long held to be inconceivable, have now passed into science as uncontested truths."

"Antiquity is the home of the Supernatural, but modern criticism reduces the Supernatural to the natural." Those who so speak favour us with instruction how "to retain the Bible, and give up the Supernatural." The perplexing signs concerning Gideon and the Fleece—perplexing and almost incredible if taken literally—are made very easy if we eliminate the miraculous, and regard them as later versions of some early metaphorical expressions recording how, when all other men of Israel were imbued with terror, the hero Gideon was full of valour; and when Israel was heated with over-confidence, Gideon alone retained coolness of judgment.

There will be no occasion thus to separate God from nature, Inspiration from Holy Scripture, and the marvellous from our Faith, if we can show that belief in the miracles of the Bible is reasonable.

Locke, a good reasoner, said—"Miracles well attested do not only find credit themselves, but give it also to other truths which need such confirmation"—the truths taught by Moses, by the Prophets, by Jesus Christ, needed such confirmation; and it was given.

Locke is contradicted by Spinoza, who asserts that miracles cannot make known the existence of God; but seeing that Spinoza regarded miracles simply as anomalies, beginning and ending with themselves; and overlooked or refused the fact that they instrumentally denote and signify Divine Will; most men will agree with Locke.

Neander says truly—"The miracle, by displaying phenomena out of the ordinary connection of cause and effect, manifests the appearance of a higher power, and points out a higher connection, in which even the chain of phenomena in the visible world must be taken up."

Our own opinion is that miracles are to be regarded sacramentally: outward and visible signs of the Almighty's invisible presence; and are meant to assure the beholder of the Divinity of the holy truths which are taught by Inspired men. Miracles, of which we obtain knowledge by testimony, are objects of faith; and, being wrought in proof of a Divine Revelation, are evidence in confirmation of faith.

The miracles of Scripture being in connection with spiritual truths—themselves great and marvellous as the miracles, mutually illustrate and confirm one another. Miracles being that material hand-writing, or incarnation, which—uniting spiritual truth with substantial reality—are essentially and substantially the word and work of God: operating, as of old, in creation; and symbolizing yet greater future marvels in the new creation. Some of the truths are as much above the capacity of our unaided intellect to acquire sure knowledge of, as the miracles are above the ordinary powers of nature to accomplish. In the confirmation and elucidation which each affords to the other, stability of material foundation is given to spiritual truth ; matter is proved to be not an evil, but a Divine thing ; and we may say—Two worlds are knit into one. We might, for example, doubt for ever concerning the likeness of man to God, or as to the Forgiveness of Sin, or as to the general Resurrection ; if we had not the miracles of Christ's Incarnation, Atonement, and Rising from the Dead, affording sign-material and sign-manual as to these very things. It seems, therefore, reasonable in the highest degree that men whose transcendentability, was laid hold of by the power of God, and carried to higher summits of sacred truth than that of any others of the human race, whether aided or unaided, could attain, should be able to verify and to certify, by means of physical evidence, that they had not been carried away from reality by ecstatic flights of fancy. It is not less reasonable, or credible, that men who are proved by the mark they have made in the world to be the greatest of mankind ; men who scale the heights of spirit, and move the depths of matter ; should have possessed that discernment of character which enabled them to commit the record and testimony of their thought and work to those whose accuracy and manner of relation should preserve the supernatural character of both.

Further—Faith means eyesight and insight. The divorce of ethereal from sublunary things is disallowed by science : marvels are reciprocal, and exist in both.

The rainbow, formed in the sky out of a dripping cloud, is made here below with a jet of water. In reasonable use of mental power, we ascend by increasing heights of conception until we attain a spiritual view of God; and by strenuous faithful effort to realize His holiness in our life we form an approximately true image of Him in our soul. As lower processes of mental thought and imagery conduct poetic genius to those high flights of which other men are incapable, so the sacred genius is led and elevated to the Seer's transcendental vision: thus natural processes are akin to the Supernatural. It is more reasonable to believe, even taking the materialist view, "Nature governs everything," that the intellectual and moral character of early men was impressed and developed by means of experimental training; than that they possessed, intuitively, such high understanding of Spiritual and Divine Mysteries that later men could never rise to the ancient level.

Have we not, even now, to think of human love in its purity, of fatherhood in highest excellency, and thence arise to conceptions of the Divine Nature? Do we not still require some outward act to conduct us, as by a sign, to the inner and spiritual? Take this experience:—We walk along the cliff of some rock-bound coast; and, as we look down at the waves breaking far below, the sunny play and our own health and strength place human aspirations in harmony with beautiful nature. Then, as we think that one false step would cast us where not all the skill of men could save, a feeling grows that we are under the care of Him who rules the world. Months or years afterwards, when asleep, or walking through crowded streets, our imagination pictures the rock-bound coast, roaring sea beneath with musical rhythm in the breakers, and memory cries—" More than all this art thou: a very child of God." No adequate scientific explanation—many have been attempted—can be given as to the origin of such thoughts in ancient days, and their continuance in modern times, unless it takes outward realities as a material platform by means of which our inner nature seeks, finds, and rejoices in the Source of both.

It seems reasonable, and part of natural fitness and harmony, that external things should co-operate with our own internal action; so that by advice of each we acquire the Reason or Cause of Both. Now this operation, the blending of the inner and outer, while a perfectly natural linking, is not less transcendental and inexplicable in its reality, than the linking, of which we are equally conscious, that gives real and high cognition, amounting almost to intuition, of the Supernatural or Universal. Lord Bacon partly expressed the thought—" God hath framed the mind of man as a glass capable of the universal world (joying to receive the signature thereof) as the eye is of light."

The world is not mere show and seeming, though it teems with perplexities: every puzzle is a beneficent parable for our intellect. There was at least something of truth in the thought of St. Francis of Assisi, that the whole of nature is a choir of God's angelic ministers. Any way it gives a touch of genius, so that even dry scientific mechanical processes have life in them. We behold that every one of the ends subserved by mechanical, chemical, and vital processes, limits some other; becomes, in turn, further means; until we rise

Is Belief in Miracles Unreasonable? 51

from brute force and cunning to manly strength and intelligence—to love morality and worship. Music suggests other and higher harmonies than those of sound. Seed-time and harvest tell, even though we refuse to listen, of another sowing, of another reaping. The host of heaven speaks in accents of terror to some of us; yet to most the heavenly vision is of Beings good and kind. Many men ceasing to think where reflection properly begins, and failing to recognize in nature that unconscious activity of reason out of which our intelligence has sprung, never attain the real height of argument. No working is by blind force: nature, viewed in inmost and uttermost significance, is a system thoroughly worked out; and the gleams of inward and outward splendour focus in our self-consciousness. No thoughtful man takes a pig-stye view; we all prefer that of the artist, well-nigh absorbed in beauty, who, not losing unity and self-control, finds an exceeding broad commandment for the spirit. We love the poet—passionate, sensuous too—finding fragrance and beauty more ethereal than the scent and colour of the lily. The amplitude of sky, the faces of children, those breathings and sweet sacred influences which are like the breath of angels, have more reason in their nature, and more history in their work, than the unpoetic think.

> "'Twas a lovely thought to mark the hours,
>   As they floated in light away,
> By the opening and the folding flowers,
>   That laugh on the summer's day.
> Yet is not life, in its real flight,
>   Mark'd thus—even thus—on earth,
> By the closing of one hope's delight,
>   And another's gentle birth?

> Oh ! let us live so that flower by flower,
>   Shutting in turn, may leave
> A lingering still for the sunset hour,
> A charm for the shaded eve."
>
> Mrs. Hemans.

Those who deny the existence of spirit, endeavour to explain the sense of mystery, the longing for true holiness, and the persuasion of a future life, as vague influences and aspirations which possess no reality. If these men are right we do wrong in following the steps of the noblest and purest of our race. The strength that filled the saints and martyrs of the Church, the Divinity that breathed in the life of Christ, was a false strength derived from delusion, was a phantom or ghost of a misconception as to the essence of things. Will any man of common-sense present the theory that the Holiness which arises in us as we endeavour to be like God, that the Faith which grows in us as we become more intimate with Christ, that the Hope which cheers us more and more as we are persuaded of the Life to Come, are mere hallucinations? Do we not reasonably maintain that there is something to be learned outside the laboratory and dissecting-room, that there are other alphabets and grammars than those of physical science? If so, as nothing can exceed its own nature—whether material, intellectual, or emotional; as no man can put himself on the top-shelf by tugging at his own waist-band; that which enables us to look beyond nature to the Supernatural, from matter to Spirit, from mortality to Immortality, must be a something within ourselves and in nature which excels both. This thought represents a fact—credible, reasonable, probable—it is a miracle; and the miracle is one of the most beautiful and

Is Belief in Miracles Unreasonable? 53

natural things in the world. Take Shakespeare's words and give them highest fulfilment as to meaning by application to Jesus Christ, and to ourselves :—

> "The idea of His Life shall sweetly creep,
> Into our study of imagination,
> And every lovely organ of His Life
> Shall come apparelled in more precious habit,
> More moving-delicate, and full of life,
> Into the eye and prospect of our souls
> Than when He lived indeed."

In connection with the fact that by Sacred Studies of Imagination—not fictitious, but Experimental Studies on the Life of Christ—we erect a spiritual statue of the Supreme in our heart ; take a great physical truth. The whole multitude of human beings who have lived on earth since the origination of mankind, are really existing in this person and in that person at the present time: in the sagacious statesman, the sublime philosopher, the poetic genius, the heroic soldier. Every particle of the ancient substance becomes new, and all past experience is the mould in which every present human habit is cast, in order to be further moulded and refashioned. The thought is good, the fact true as wonderful, though pantheists abuse it : we behold a marvellous simultaneous existence in the world. It is perfectly natural, but who can explain the guiding of the line, the separate personality, individuality, identity, that we feel ; and do it in conformity with the other verity, that we are only as microscopic atoms in the wondrous whole? The invisible, the pre-existent, enter the visible and present ; so that all the past possesses a future, and the like must be affirmed of the present.

On the physical truth erect a spiritual reality. The spirit—the thought, the soul, the genius, the mind, the true man—of all that multitude passed not away any more than the bodily substance. If we track matter to the edge of an incomprehensible truth, no less can be done with regard to that most excellent thing in matter which confers highest value. The system of matter exists in a region of space; that which we call the spirit, dwelling in matter, takes possession of space by means of matter; but the intensity and true life of it cannot be expressed in terms of space. We are in the infancy of thought and language: we can only say—that which we call spirit is not to be defined by locality—as a part of infinitude; but, rather, by inwardness of a different extension—the eternal. This fact—duly blended with the diversity of nature in locality as to Infinitude, and in time as to Eternity—will serve to take off the edge of unbelief as to the miraculous.

Thus rightly using our reason, by endeavouring to raise it into high exercise, we find that nature borders everywhere on the Supernatural. The commonest things contain germs of the wonderful. Every moment of our life, every particle of our body, every vibration of our substance, enters the transcendental. Space extends into Infinitude, time has some alliance with Eternity, the human spirit yearns for the Divine Spirit. Reason has shown its strength, become its own critic, and found design and process in nature—wonderful and subtle, powerful and grand. Design on a grander scale than that of an artificer constructing a machine; process more wonderful than the growth of a universal tree; conducting worlds in new paths, replenishing them with new operations—ever springing and advancing; containing everywhere indications of a larger future knowledge for the intelligent, and promises to the pure in heart of wider rule in the manifold dominions of the Almighty.

THOUGHT VIII.

ARE MIRACLES UNNATURAL?

"Dei Voluntas rerum natura est."
St. Augustine.

THOUGHT has made it clear—that nature derives its origin and continuance from the Supernatural. It is certain that things were not always as they now are. To admit this, however, brings in the miraculous; and, though by our process of reasoning, miracles assume an air of probability and reasonableness, they are nevertheless asserted to be somewhat unnatural—contrary to the fixed course of things; and may therefore be refused.

The refusal is unwise. The miraculous is not more Supernatural than is nature itself. As to fixed order of things, elasticity is more remarkable and prevalent than fixity. The same things even are not always done in the same way; and if miracles are a sort of by-path in connection with the common highway, a kind of relief to uniformity and denial of fatality, they become instructive lessons in natural variety. The point of contact with Divine energy seems near and direct in the miracle, more distant and by manifold media in the natural, but in reality the energy in both cases is nigh at hand.

The thought may be enlarged :—

When we regard external objects, and consider the operation of forces, we are never able to discover any essential power or quality which binds the antecedent to the event, cause to effect: rendering the one an infallible sequence of the other. At the first appearance of an object we cannot guess at the effect which will result. Solidity, extension, motion, are known only by experience; and these qualities are so complete in themselves that we can never point out any other event that necessarily results from them. The scenes of nature are continually shifting, one object follows another, but the energy actuating the whole is hidden— never reveals itself in any of the qualities of matter. Heat attends flame, but we do not know their connection; nor can any simple instance of the operation of bodies impart the idea of power; no bodies so displaying power as to give us an original idea of it.

Unthinking people imagine that the fall of heavy bodies, the growth of plants, the nourishment of animals, are by the very energy that seems connected with the effect; and when custom has allied the antecedent to the consequent the belief arises, and then the strong assurance, that the two are and must always be joined together: but there is no visible tie between them, no necessary idea of power or union between any two ideas of the mind, or any two operations of bodies, other than that arising from their ordinary connection or transition. Hence those who speak of miracles being contrary to nature are in fairy land, have no line to fathom the immense abysses they pretend to skip over so lightly: all that they can say is—"Miracles do not fall in with that usual order and sequence in nature with which we are personally acquainted."

We will now, as by experiment, verify the reasoning.

Lucretius, with somewhat of oracular solemnity, predicted—and modern physicists, because of remarkable facts and analogies in nature, assert—the dissolution of all things. "Suppose all authors in all languages agree that from the 1st of January, 1600, there was a total darkness over the whole earth for eight days: suppose that the tradition of this extraordinary event is still strong and lively among the people: that all travellers who return from foreign countries bring us accounts of the same tradition, without the least variation or contradiction: it is evident that our present philosophers, instead of doubting the fact, ought to receive it as certain, and ought to search for the causes whence it might be derived. The decay, corruption, and dissolution of nature are an event rendered probable by so many analogies that any phenomenon which seems to have a tendency towards that catastrophe comes within the reach of human testimony." (Hume's "Essay on Miracles.") From the above we learn that the end of the world is a matter of likelihood. If it come at all, it may come in a moment—at any moment: up to that moment the argument of experience will continue in full force, but in a moment it will be exploded. The argument derived from experience as to the continuance of things in their present form and order of existence utterly fails then in disproof of miracles. There is no reason why a new event should be in the course, or like the hitherto manner, of nature: therefore, unlikeness is not unreasonable—is not unnatural.

Are Miracles Unnatural?

What is meant by the order of nature? That succession and recurrence of physical events of which we have experience. This leaves out that of which we have no experience; and the assumption that nature in the past was, and that nature in the future will be, like that of which we have knowledge, is based on an unwarrantable expectation of likeness. Experience can give direct and certain information of those precise objects only, and of that precise time, which fall under its cognizance; but what connection has it with past and future time, and with other objects? The inference of connection is not linked by reason to the fact—it is a mere supposition. Hume ("Enquiry concerning the Human Understanding," Sect. IV.) says—"Let the course of things be allowed hitherto ever so regular, that alone, without some new argument or inference, proves not for the future that it will continue so. As an agent, I am quite satisfied on the point, but as a philosopher I want to learn the foundation of the inference. No reading nor enquiry has yet been able to remove my difficulty." The inference from the present to the past and to the future is not linked by reason; therefore we may infer the contrary without collision of reason; consequently the invariable succession and recurrence of physical events with which we are acquainted, is no proof of invariable succession and recurrence of events and times with which we are unacquainted—is no proof that miracles are unnatural.

Nature can only prevent miracles by enforcing that order, and the continuance of those events, with which we are acquainted; but science proclaims that there is no such power of causation in nature, we are only acquainted with antecedents and consequents. The highly vaunted chain of nature, with which unbelievers thought to bind miracles and prevent their going forth, is proved to be a rope of sand: miracles march as strong men valiant for the Most High. If there are persons so defective in the choice intellectual and noble practical part of human character that they cannot persuade themselves, let them at least remember that it is as easy for them to be in error, as it is for the world to lie in wickedness. God's cabinets may open only for jewels His secrets are made known but to few friends, even as the Spirit's whispers are heard distinctly and regarded by none but the holy. Some creatures spin and toil, yet have no understanding; there are understandings which neither spin nor toil, yet Solomon in all his glory was not arrayed like one of them. He who hath eyesight and insight will discern the miracle.

A miracle is not so much contrary to nature, or unnatural, or a suspension of nature, as a superinduced nature. It is no violation of nature for a man to roll away a stone: why may not an angel roll one from a sepulchre? The physician, by skill and means known to himself, cures a patient of fever; why should not Jesus, with greater skill and higher means, heal cases much more dangerous? The miracle is indeed a manifestation that a portion of our world is drawn into and within a higher order of things, of more extensive range and power, in which are effected displacings and arrangings and elevations: even as at the advent of man nature was put, by human skill and power, to unwonted, higher, and till then unimaginable uses.

Ignorance of the cause of miracles and the manner

of their operation is not sufficient reason for their refusal. There are many physical events which cannot be physically investigated, nor can one be examined so fully that we attain essential knowledge of it, or are able to exclude the miraculous from it. Some miracles are wrought by means partly known, for example, the Deluge—" The fountains of the great deep being broken up, and the windows of heaven opened." These figurative words indicate a natural operation. The miracle exists in the synchronism of nature's operations with the time appointed, so as to be subservient to the Divine Counsels. "God, looking upon His own Omnipotence, knows all possibilities, looking upon His own Determinations, He sees all futurities; looking upon His own Wisdom, He beholds all varieties, all degrees and differences of being; which yet put not forth the least shadow of difference in Him."

We have reason to believe that the known course of nature is not the only course. There are sports in plants, eccentricities in animals, anomalies everywhere, subordination of lower to higher, two-sidedness and two-foldedness. There is the riddle of life, the greater puzzle of mind, the surpassing mystery of responsibility, elevating pre-existing matter and force into nobler substance and higher energy, until human consciousness receives, retains, and reflects a truth—God created the world "in gloriam suam" and "in salutem nostram;" for which there can be no other rational interpretation than that it is true: God did create the world for His own glory and for our welfare. The material universe is the complement of intellect. We understand, by reception and use, that mighty holy influence which in the case of opponents casts them down—as the band was stricken and fell in the presence of Jesus; which in the case of true though erring men, like Peter, and James, and John, puts new life in them, prepares new life for them, and makes them leaders of the world; and truly by the works of such men, the world's original men, God's chosen men, the earth is a world and not a waste; and the most blessed marvels are true miracles, yet wonderfully natural!

THOUGHT IX.

COSMICAL AND MENTAL ANALOGIES.

"There is a correspondence between things spiritual and things natural, and by means of this correspondence their conjunction takes place."

VAST and various as are the worlds, though nature presents so many strange and unexpected combinations and results, it is a striking fact that marvellous unity underlies the diversity. So all-prevailing is the unity that the very strangest occurrences, even things which appear impossible to common experience, are actually verified by ordinary scientific knowledge, and in a manner wonderfully simple. The thought naturally arises, that whatever in miraculous operation is abnormal, apparently capricious, and subversive of other laws, will probably, in some degree, be represented in nature's ordinary course; so that we find cosmical and mental analogies, scientific surprises, and physical catastrophes, akin to the miraculous. We try to verify the thought.

The suspension of gravity possesses analogy and permanence in the law of diffusion of gases. The diffusion is not more capable of scientific explanation than are the ancient marvels. Make an experiment:—Hydrogen is the lightest body known. Take a bottle of it, and by means of a narrow glass tube connect it vertically with a bottle of oxygen—a much heavier gas, the oxygen being below. The oxygen, despite the action of gravity, will ascend: a complete mixture of the two gases in both bottles being the result. Other examples are afforded by the chemical combination of light bodies which become heavier in the process, and of heavier bodies which become lighter. That the natural marvels are permanent, but that the miracles were temporary, renders the former more advantageous as abiding witnesses and symbols of the latter.

Isomerism, a term applied to bodies containing the same elements, united in the same proportions, but differing in their physical, physiological, and chemical properties, carries us into the midst of marvels most surprising in character. We need not, therefore, be greatly surprised when the Bible states, that things possessing the same elements, in like number and proportions, may so differ, through some hidden natural or supernatural process, that their physical, chemical, and physiological properties remain permanently dissimilar.

Electricity and magnetism are full of mysteries. Take a cube, or sphere of copper, suspend it by a twisted cord; so that it be made to spin, by untwisting, between the poles of an excited electro-magnet. It experiences the retardation due to friction only; but, on the supervention of the magnetic force, the rotation is suddenly arrested. Faraday showed by an interesting experiment, that in passing a plate of copper rapidly to and fro between the magnetic poles, you seem to be cutting cheese though nothing is visible: space becomes as if it were a kind of solid.

Various miracles of preservation, and of destruction,

have natural analogies in the preservation of ice amidst flame, in the ignition of phosphoretted hydrogen at ordinary temperature, the burning of air in coal-gas, in combustion proceeding without flames, and in those experiments by which light is extracted from darkness, and heat from cold.

Changes, utterly incomprehensible in the nature of things, have many natural analogies:—

Phosphorus may be yellow, or white like porcelain, or black, or red. In the clear transparent form it is yellow, soft, a wax-like body, tasteless; but, in solution, it is of a sharp pungent flavour. Common phosphorus, melted and then suddenly cooled to 32° F., becomes black. The yellow is made of a dull red colour, without taste and odour, by heating in an atmosphere in which it cannot oxidize. The red variety is not poisonous. All the others are active poisons. Oxygen, sustainer of life, and the great burner up of dead organic matter, is—when compressed—the most fearful poison known. Sulphur, when separated from a compound at the positive pole of the battery, is soluble in carbonic disulphide; when separated at the negative pole of the battery, it is insoluble in carbonic disulphide. Heated to 280° F., it becomes liquid; continue and increase the heat to 350° F., then it is so thick and viscid that it will not fall from the inverted vessel. At from 350° to 500° F., the fluidity is restored, and it takes a dull brown colour. Pour it then into cold water and the elastic variety is produced. In cooling it passes inversely through the same stages; becoming viscous, then fluid, and finally solid.

Allotropism, or the capability of compound bodies,

F

having the same percentage and molecular composition, of existing in more than one shape, finds startling and surpassing examples amongst the old marvels. There are manifold changes in the nature of things which science can only register, not explain.

Accounts of falling stones, darkness and light, sudden appearances of stars, are exemplified in the fall of aërolites, in the October and November meteors, in the various mysterious darknesses related in the history of astronomy; in the appearances, disappearances, and blazings forth of stars into splendour, of which there are many historic records. We could greatly enlarge the account of these analogies, but forbear. Some of them are permanent, others are periodic, some of frequent, others of rare occurrence. They are not explanations of miracles, but exhibitions of variety, startling and extensive, in which nature falls not far short of the miraculous. "There are more things in heaven and earth than are dreamt of in our philosophy;" and we are wise in maintaining that there is a possibility of phenomena which, though seeming altogether opposed to the Laws of Physics or of Physiology, do not so much oppose as transcend them.

Miracles of other kinds have their similitude in those startling but natural changes by which things similar become dissimilar. In chemical combination, for example, we obtain effects which bear no resemblance sensibly, chemically, physically, or physiologically, to the constituent elements. Indeed we have no means of estimating the force of affinity absolutely, and very uncertain means of estimating it relatively. Like will consort with like, or will refuse; negatives will agree, or differ yet more. Strychnia, a deadly poison, is formed by the combination of those harmless bodies—carbon, hydrogen, oxygen, and nitrogen. Sulphuric acid, a corrosive poison, is formed by the combination of those inert bodies—sulphur, hydrogen, and oxygen. In vital action, by means of a single fluid, all the elements of growth and nutrition are elaborated, and the various secretions have their composition determined. Our awaking from sleep; and those resurrections, not uncommon, from death-like torpor and apparent insensibility; are parables of the resurrection. The miracle of raising the dead, marvellous as a new creation, is not, however, a raising of the matter constituting our old mortal body. Scripture states that those who become new men in this life have new and glorious bodies in the world to come. Personality and individuality are retained in connection with a transformation of the whole man from glory to glory.

The Bible reveals many unexpected varieties, departures from rule, the happening of unusual things, the production of great by small, *vice versâ*, and marvellous unlikelies, which have their counterpart in many interesting facts. Hydrogen is believed to be a gaseous metal, Bromine is the only liquid non-metallic element, Mercury is the only liquid metallic element, and Gallium melts by heat of the hand. Some metals are so soft that they can be indented with the nail, others can be cut with a knife. Compounds of nitrogen and oxygen, things which destroy if inspired more than a few seconds, form laughing-gas; substances become differently constituted at different pressures, become bodies stable or unstable, of great heat or intense cold. Selenium is found in various allotropic forms. Carbon is the diamond, graphite, coke, soot, lampblack, wood charcoal, animal charcoal, tinder. Probably all elements are able to assume every form of solid, fluid, gas. These varieties, existing where none were looked for ; these departures from rule where and when rule seems strictest ; production by means apparently inadequate, and the existence of the unlikely where the unlikely is almost impossible ; may be fairly counted natural features of the supernatural.

Thus, not for explaining but for illustrating miracles, we possess unusual yet natural counterparts : the natural phenomena being no more explainable than the supernatural. It may be said of some of the examples given, that they do not illustrate miracles except as showing varieties and mysteries in nature. Let it be so : then these varieties and mysteries, if somewhat enlarged, are very pictures of actual miracles. That is all we contend for. It is a fact that the same substances may and do exist in different shapes and states ; that all properties need conditions to call them forth ; and that many bodies, not all, changed from one state to another, can be changed from the second to the first. We are not to stare with dull astonishment, but to observe that these great varieties seem to have come into the world—not as things of perturbation and unnaturalness ; but to show that though the hearts of the unprepared masses are dumb and useless and irresponsive ; others, peculiar and chosen, may hear a voice, know of laws, and be so attuned to spiritual music, that they fashion their souls to partake of new potencies, new laws, new stages, which form part of the grand universal plan of teleological development now operating in the universe.

Those not in the habit of looking into things, so as to discern inner meaning and power, do not discover the marvellously knit purpose and complicate process by which mountains are raised, crumbled, dissolved, and carried into the sea. They see no mystery in the dew and rain and cloud, nor find anything wonderful in the continuous and general operations of nature—though marvellous indeed. They may, however, learn of the mystery and miracles by the fact that every vital process forming an organism, and every mental exercise, is more wonderful and artistic than any operation by poet, or painter, or sculptor. Watch the marble under the artist's hands, as blow by blow, and touch by touch, with power, with skill, the dead substance seems to live in the perfect image of manly strength or feminine beauty. The vital process—the mental process—in human nature, constructs in manner more exquisite, by operation more mysterious, with plan more felicitous, with result more wonderful, the embryo—the child—the man. Not a dead form, as the marble; but a living creature with life in every portion of the substance. Not insensible to feeling, nor incapable of thought, as the statue; but instinct with sensation, intelligence, emotion. Think of the process as completed, internal and external, at that time when the Glory of the Lord shall replenish the Earth : when pure light shines everywhere, and every life, heart, and intellect, amidst gladness and righteousness, loves, serves, and praises the Almighty. That will be a great miracle. We have the promise and symbol in every man who now tries unfeignedly to do the will of God perfectly.

Doubtless, there are men who overcome the world; who have the inspiration that made martyrs mighty; men who live and walk with God. The marvels surrounding them, or wrought by them, or performed on their behalf, are not disturbances of nature or unnatural; but means and processes preparing for and prophesying of things to come. They are indications that the present and physical nature of things is not eternally fixed; that material existence is not unchangeable; and that time is simply, in abstract, a relation of position between states of consciousness. Even the phenomena which accompany certain morbid conditions of the brain furnish analogous examples. De Quincey states that in some of his dreams—"The sea appeared to him paved with innumerable forms, supplicating, wrathful, or despairing; rising in myriads, in generations, for ages; that, again, an imaginary architecture was pictured to him in vivid and unsupportable splendour, capable of increasing in size and infinite reproduction." Sometimes he seemed to live fifty or one hundred years in a single night; he had feelings which seemed to last a thousand years, or rather for a lapse of time which exceeded the limits of human experience.

The preceding statements appear to be without flaw: miracles have cosmical and mental analogies; lay aside their apparent unreasonableness and unnaturalness in finding a law within the law; and explain themselves by an inner sense. They seem to be special vivid pictures of quick painting by the master to represent the process by which the things seen were made of those which do not appear; and the process by which they will become other than they now are. We, ourselves, in the faculty and consciousness of sometimes living apart from the body—both in imagination and in dreams—find that causes have two faces: effect is not only produced by the mind, but by the mind joined with the body.

As for Mind, even the heroes of the world generally know but one or two spiritual truths mightily, of which they have both eyesight and insight; not mere opinion, but certainty. To them, however, the meanest flower that blows comes as a messenger from God. They share "the larger æther and the purple light" with which the Supernatural clotheth all things. We cast our lot in with these heroes, not with those who would make our life but a dim and dusky stage, with all the sweet Eden-garden scenes and fair heavenly perspective thrust out of sight.

> " We trust we have not wasted breath :
> We think we are not wholly brain—
> Magnetic mockeries—nor in vain,
> Like Paul with beasts, we fight with Death;
>
> " Nor only cunning casts in clay;
> Let science prove we are, and then
> What matters science unto men,
> At least to us? We still would pray !"
>
> *In Memoriam.*

THOUGHT X.

MIRACLES ARE CREDIBLE.

"A miracle is a violation of the laws of nature; and, as a firm and unalterable experience has established these laws, the proof against a miracle, from the very nature of the fact, is as entire as any argument from experience can possibly be imagined."—DAVID HUME.

THE above statement is an example of the narrowness wrought in the minds of men who, habitually refusing the miraculous, train themselves as professed sceptics.

That a miracle does not agree with the usual course of antecedent and sequence that most men have experience of is true; but that our present experience of natural order is the essential and only one is not true—is utterly false; for, and we must repeat in other words what we have said before, we know about as well as we can know most scientific facts, that existing antecedents and effects arose out of a state of things altogether at variance with the present state. Hence, so far from science proving that miracles are incredible because they are a violation of nature, the existing order of things is proved to be itself miraculous; because arising out of a previous, and, as compared with the present, an unnatural condition.

To talk of our firm and unalterable experience of

laws being proof that no other men had a variable experience, is equal to the absurdity of saying that our experience and knowledge cover all possible experience and knowledge. Vary Hume's argument, but use his words—"There must be an uniform experience against every miraculous event, otherwise the event would not merit that appellation. And as an uniform experience amounts to a proof, there is here a direct and full proof, from the nature of the fact, against the existence of any miracles; nor can such proof be destroyed, or the miracle rendered credible, but by an opposite proof, which is superior."

The fallacy is threefold; 1, in the assumption that all experience is uniform; 2, that uniform partial experience is universal; 3, that our exceptional experience as to the miraculous must be superior to our so called uniform experience concerning nature's ordinary course.

1. There is no such thing as uniform experience. Those who possess the largest acquaintance with nature know of so many startling surprises, that whatever comes within the range of possibility cannot be regarded as wholly improbable.

2. Even were our own experience uniform, that would not measure nor fix the limits of the actual to other men, in other times, in other circumstances. All the present inhabitants of the world might say—"We have not seen a miracle, not one of us has been present at any time, in any place where a miracle was wrought"—but their evidence is of no avail against that of the few trustworthy intelligent capable men who were present in the place and at the time and did see that a miracle was wrought.

3. "Miracles cannot be rendered credible, but by an opposite proof which is superior." If it be required that the few alleged miracles, which a small number of men declare that they have witnessed, be rendered credible by proof derived from an experience as large as that of the many who have not seen a miracle, the requirement is unreasonable. We, nevertheless, as if to verify the assertion—The impossible is the only thing which is sure to happen, assay to give the required proof:—

The absolutely invariable experience of men is that they are unable to attain actual cognition of causes, can only know things as antecedents and consequents. The cause of the simplest as of the greatest events is inscrutable. We do not know the cause of gravity, nor of electricity, nor of light, nor of heat, nor of life, nor of intelligence. So far from being able to give a natural account of them, that is to explain their origin, or to afford reasons for their continuance; the whole are wrapped in mystery interpenetrated and pierced by energies of which we only know that we know nothing. Consequently, the universal experience of men, qualified to judge, is—that the whole of nature is a marvel, and every, even the commonest, event miraculous. Where all is miraculous, the existence and use of by-paths for unwonted use of wonted and unwonted energies, is but a small variety of marvel. Thus we establish miracle by evidence commensurate with the experience of mankind.

Opponents may endeavour to take off the edge of our argument by the assertion—"Nothing is accounted a miracle if it ever happen in the common course of nature." It seems a little silly, if the foundation of everything is miraculous, to deny the existence of that variety in operation which really seems needed to rescue the common course from being accounted a fated course. Moreover, as to these peculiar or separate events, it is a matter of fact that nature cannot explain its own origin; and as the nature we are acquainted with had origin in a state not like the present, the existence of these other miracles is no great marvel; they too arise out of an unlike state, are an example of continuance as to the old marvellous work, and bind miraculous variety into marvellous unity.

We now enter the moral argument. David Hume shall state a case :—" When any one tells me that he saw a dead man restored to life, I immediately consider with myself whether it be more probable that this person should either deceive or be deceived, or that the fact which he relates should really have happened. I weigh the one miracle against the other; and according to the superiority which I can discover, I pronounce my decision, and always reject the greater miracle. If the falsehood of his testimony would be more miraculous than the event which he relates, then, and not till then, can he pretend to command my belief or opinion."

Here again is the fatal fallacy which assumes that the rareness and marvellous nature of an event are an argument against the good faith and intelligence of the witnesses. Want of experience in the many, the ignorance of those not present at the time, nor in the place of the rare occurrence, are to avail against the positive accurate knowledge and experience of those who were present. The many ignorant and treacherous men who brought about the crucifixion of Jesus, and who did not see Him after the resurrection, are to be believed rather than the honest upright and intelligent five hundred who, with the apostles, constantly affirmed that He had risen from the dead. Materialists on the evidence of a bone, or part of one, or even the impression of it made in old time in clay or sand, firmly believe in creatures which they have never seen; it is but a fraction of his knowledge that a scientific man can verify; the greater part must rest on testimony; yet, a few of these men, knowing as they do, that, *a priori*, no argument can be set up against the existence of unexpected and unimagined forms of life and energy, assert that miracles, though but unusual manifestations of energy, are, *a priori*, so incredible that no scientific man will give even a momentary consideration to the evidence.

We now advance to a brief statement of the facts which prove that the existence of miracles is a lesser marvel than their non-existence would be.

I. We are all conscious of a tendency towards the marvellous, not only have pleasure when our surprise and wonder are excited, but possess a deep conviction that this tendency and these emotions are an essential part of our inner nature, and correspond to something without. From earliest times, in the rude pre-historic memorials of worship witnessing amongst all nations, barbarous and civilized, there is proof of ineradicable conviction as to the reality of that whence various supernatural events proceed.

II. Many spurious miracles having been detected, fanatics being so ready to lie, heated imaginations leading to credulity, and possession of supernatural gifts conferring a splendid and desirable halo of renown, men of prudence in all ages rightly refused credit, so far as possible, to whatever opposed common custom and experience. Not because they were unbelieving as to miracles; but that in due use of their power, intelligence, experience, they might separate the true from the false. Hence, the credulity that accepted all things without asking a question, and the sagacity demanding verification before yielding assent, alike rested on the persuasion that our world is the scene of strange but rare marvels.

III. While we refuse purposeless miracles, done in a corner, or where verification was impossible; and put away all romantic narratives coming from barbarous nations; the absolute impossibility of rationally or scientifically explaining away the universal conviction and expectation of marvels affords proof to our best thinkers that there is a substratum of reality. Indeed, barbarous men would not be barbarous if so gifted with genius and imagination that they could create an idea of God, and invent miracles as works by which He manifested Himself; nor would bad men, if they could, give the world such a volume as the Bible. This process of thought leads the ablest of our race, mathematicians, naturalists, chemists, philosophers, to accept Holy Scripture and its Miracles as really a lesser marvel, and more in accordance with the facts of human nature, than that rejection which brands universal consciousness and conviction, sublimest thought and holiest aspirations, as a delusion and a snare.

IV. These miracles are in connection with the grandest and purest system of morals in existence. They are Divine sign-manuals of doctrine, precept, ritual, sacrifice, festival, and law. They are parts of a Revelation concerning secret things of the past, and of wonders in the future, not less miraculous than the marvels inaugurating them. They belong to a mysterious scheme of Providence by which the world is to be rescued from evil, men are to be redeemed from sin, and all things are to be made new. They are object lessons in science which our physicists have not yet mastered, and indicate a wealth of unknown energies the exploration of which is not begun. They are essential elements in the only rational religion possessed by the world, and destruction of faith in them will falsify the whole of sacred history, and take conviction of its verity from the minds of all thoughtful men. They are, being Supernatural, that which proves the Bible to be a Book of God, becoming works for our Saviour the Son of God, rightly attend His Birth —the Incarnation of God, His Resurrection—a symbol of human victory over Death, His Ascension—a display of the Heavenly Pathway. They are evidence — in the wonders of the Resurrection — that the Atonement is sufficient, and the Redemption effectual. Take away miracles, then all sacred doctrine, all promises, all hopes, perish : for they are founded on miracles. Not one pure gleam would shine from the Good Land to enlighten our darkness, nothing enabling us to discern between the righteous and the wicked. That this should be so, that the Jewish scheme, knit to the Christian by a hundred ties, is a gross delusion ; that prophets and martyrs were mad ; that Moses was a juggler ; Isaiah an enthusiast ; Elijah a lunatic ; our Blessed Lord a knave ; and the

Apostles dupes; we cannot believe. It is quite true that no one, in our day, is so wicked and foolish as to say this: but what avails it for modern infidelity to exalt our Lord and the ancient prophets to the highest pitch of merely human excellence, and then to assert that those who knew them best, whose special business it was to give a true record of their words and acts, have made them the originators—we must speak plainly—of the most astounding falsehoods—made them, though true men, to fill the world with lies? The thing is incredible. Moreover, that the greatest and purest men in the world have through all ages been worshipping they know not what; regarding books as true and holy which are essentially false and wicked; and have been made truthful, chaste, heroic, and God-fearing, by that which is built on the greatest falsehoods; would be a more astounding marvel than the maddest of men ever thought of, or the most Satanic of men could devise. Such a miracle of folly, such an incredible impossible mixing of things incapable of mixture, we must reject as utterly absurd; and humbly and heartily thank God for the marvels with which He attested Revelation.

V. These miracles—possessing world-wide meaning, and ultimately to become a universal blessing—were mostly wrought in, for, and by, the men of a nation who are even now an enigma to the world. Far from being credulous, they are the most unbelieving of all races. Their history, whether in Old or New Testament, or found on modern page, is proof. They were incapable of weaving a mythical element in their records, but their annals, their literature, their great men, their national character, their whole past, their present, and all good expected in the future, are bound up with a system miraculously bestowed and confirmed. The miracles were unwillingly received, and frequently resisted; publicly wrought for the most part; and always capable of verification or of disproof. They were done amongst a race whose lives were the purest, whose laws were the justest, and whose religion was the most reasonable yet most remarkable in the world. A people wonderful for genius—not in the Hellenic sense, but in special faculty for things Divine; the only worshippers of One supreme and most holy God; a people in whom alone, so far as we can judge, resided a comprehensive continuous spirit of prophecy; and whose great men render all other human majesties of comparatively little renown. To charge them with ignorance and barbarism belittles and disgraces the false accuser. To fight against true miracles with pretended miracles; to vaunt concerning sleight-of-hand trickery, Satanic delusions, witchcrafts, sorceries, dark operations of Seekers of the Dead, that Divine Deeds may hide themselves; and, by means of hateful wicked mimicries, to discredit the real and true; were indeed to make a miracle of delusions, and to cast out the true miracle as no marvel.

The greater miracle were no miracle: and as our opponents, by their own selected system of argument, are bound to choose the lesser marvel; they must, as true men, as honest men, as reasonable men, receive the miracles recorded in Holy Scripture as credible according to all custom of thought, as confirmed by all experience of life, and as worthy of all acceptation.

THOUGHT XI.

MIRACLES ARE CAPABLE OF PROOF.

"Life exists in nature as an instrumental cause. Motion in nature is action in a living subject. Modification in nature is sensation in a living thing. What is effort in nature is will in life. What is distinction of light in nature is intellect in that which lives."—*From Note Book.*

DAVID HUME says—"A miracle can never be proved so as to be the foundation of a system of religion." Similar assertions are frequently made by men who count themselves too clever for the Common Faith. The cleverness is spoiled by a great fault—want of common sense. No man, unless partially blinded by unbelief, could make so rash and ignorant and false a statement in the face of Christianity. Christianity is founded on the Miracle of Christ's Resurrection: "If Christ be not raised your faith is vain" (1 Cor. xv. 7). This miracle confirms all other miracles, and with the Incarnation—manifesting Christ's Divine nature—gives God's own signature to our Faith: the purest, the greatest, the most marvellous Faith the world has ever possessed. To assert—"A miracle can never be proved so as to be the foundation of a system of religion—" stands convicted of grossest folly and falsity in the presence of that innumerable host of mathematicians, physicists, philosophers, and statesmen, whose science and faith have made them blessings to the world.

The following statement is a necessary inference from Hume's false premises: "Though the being to whom the miracle is ascribed, be in this case the Almighty, it does not, upon that account, become a whit more probable; since it is impossible for us to know the actions or attributes of such a Being, otherwise than from the experience which we have of his productions in the usual course of nature." ("Philosophical Works of David Hume," vol. iv. sec. 10, Miracles, p. 148, ed. 1854.) The grossness of error will be exposed by a little reflection.

We know of God in many ways: by the usual and unusual course of nature; by events which occur hourly, and by those happening only once in a century, or in a millennium. We know of God whenever and however He pleases to reveal Himself: whether in Word, or in Work. If God cannot reveal Himself to the consciousness of men, how is it that they are conscious of Him? If He cannot reveal Himself in the literature of the world, how is it that literature is full of Him? If He cannot manifest Himself in miracles and marvels, how is it that the whole world believes that He does so manifest Himself?

The usual course of nature is in no respect commonplace, but full of marvels; and these marvels are so akin to miracles that we do not know their essential cause, nor are their antecedents invariable. In that course, dead inorganic matter is fashioned into living organisms; this, day by day, is a quickening of the dead; and life is a miracle to the dead. Sleep is like death, and waking from sleep is newness of life; sleeping and awaking are a figurative dying and living in the same day; and not the less marvellous because so common. There are times when men breathe not, and the pulse is still; when coldness of the flesh, and absence of all vital functions, seem to prove that life is departed. The physician says—"Dead," but the man is alive. Resurrections are not uncommon. Men of common sense, those of uncommon sense too, regard them as hinting of that great revival when men, returned to inorganic matter, shall come back as living organisms of a wonderful spiritual nature: for the most exalted consciousness and the most elevated phenomena are the effects of a complication which has come out of the simplest elements.

As to knowing of God by His works, we can and do know. We know Him, bringing the visible from the invisible, as by Creation; by fashioning all things—as were He an Architect; by the painting of natural pictures—as were He an Artist; by making of organisms —as were He a wonderful Mechanic; by quickening into life—Himself being the Source of it. Every Theist probably allows this; yet every one of these operations, whether wrought indirectly by means, or directly without means, is miraculous. Further—we know God as so fashioning our frame that we are consciously His children; and we think that as parents communicate to offspring their own nature, disposition, faculties, and character; our sense of Divine life, love for, and desire to please Divinity, are a wonderful heredity.

Some Materialists answer—"Cause must be proportioned to the effect; and if we exactly and precisely proportion it, we shall never find in it any qualities which point further, or afford an inference concerning any other design and performance." This is a pretentious and erroneous saying: for we know neither the whole of any cause, nor the whole of any effect. Take it thus, and the error is seen at once—a hundred ton steam-hammer cracks a nut, if we exactly and precisely apportion the cause to the effect we shall never find any qualities in the steam-hammer which point further, or afford an inference concerning any other design or performance. In like manner, we find antecedents and consequents in nature which go beyond nature; we may acquire in this life approximate notions of the life to come; and it is possible to ascend from created things to their Creator. Our ideas of nature are not necessarily and solely those of mechanical effect; they partake of that enlargement which life, intelligence, and moral responsibility bestow. The small eye of our body discerns the infinitude of space, and the eye of our understanding looks upon many glorious mental worlds. The present life may well be likened to a window whence we look into the future; and we are sure that future—physically, mentally, and morally—will be the sum total of the past, with other things added. We learn from nature itself, that the course of things is frequently altered; that no two things, nor any one thing in any two moments of time, are precisely alike; yet the modern doctrine concerning continuance of energy warrants our conviction that the unknown is connected with the known, and somewhat like—with other things added. We do not frame a religious hypothesis to account for natural events, do not look wholly backward while we argue forward, but use all our knowledge to attain and do attain certainty, that the whole course of nature is a passage to something further: a continuous development into other and higher forms of being, the continuity never being a drear and dead uniformity, but ever and ever intersected by marvellous changes. This, in essence, is miraculous.

The argument is capable of physical verification:—

We knew long ago that in a vacuum a column of water would ascend to the height of thirty-two feet—not higher. Torricelli thought about this; took a glass tube, a yard in length, closed at one end, open at the other, and filled it with mercury; then, stopping the open end with his thumb, inverted it in a vessel filled with the liquid metal. He had the joy to find his thought realized in a fact never before revealed to human eyes. Every village pump is a proof of Torricelli's genius. The celebrated Pascal took up the fact, and reasoned—If the mercurial column be supported by the atmosphere, the higher we ascend in the air the lower the column will sink as the weight overhead is decreased. He experimented, and the Barometer was discovered. Kepler, by many observations of planetary motions, ascertained their order, and gave a general expression of them in what are known as "Kepler's Laws." We can retrace the past motions of planets, and foresee the future; ascertain the position of stars at any time; and we know that perturbations and apparent anomalies establish more firmly the dominion of law. Newton marshalled his thoughts around the grand fact—Gravitation; and virtually, weighed the moon. As a result and verification of all this previous thinking, we can, when perturbations are detected in planetary motions, indicate the region where the disturbing influence may be discovered; and the practical astronomer, turning thitherward his telescope, beholds, say, Neptune in the predicted place. We marvellously pass from ignorance, behold "the future in the instant," know the coming place and state of worlds. The underlying essence of the knowledge is marvellous in its nature, and the germ of something still more wonderful.

The Materialist takes hold of the knowledge, and thus perverts it—"Because laws, so far as science observes, are invariable and continue for ever; there is nothing to indicate that their operation has ever been suspended, or ever been crossed by Divine spontaneous action; or that a state of things at any time existed that could not rigorously be deduced from the preceding state."

The inaccuracy of all such general assertions, professing to know everything, may nearly always be seen by a reversal of the assumed fact, thus—Laws, so far as science observes, are not invariable; even the action of gravity varies with the increase of distance, and is at last inappreciable. It is continually interfered with, interrupted, and rendered ineffective, by vital and mental action. All the Facts of science show not only that the operation of existing laws has been suspended, but that the laws themselves, if we extend them to all time—past and future, remain intelligible for a finite period only; and then indicate, as to the past, a state of things which could not have resulted under known laws. Thus, as the present points unanimously to a beginning, so there may be, and probably are to be,

Miracles are Capable of Proof. 87

future states of things, incapable of derivation by known laws—of tangible matter and its energy—from any, to us, conceivable present arrangement. Indeed, when we know most, we are most conscious of a deeper depth as to our ignorance ; and are led to seek higher aid in all that most nearly concerns our well-being.

Concerning the variety underlying laws apparently invariable, take the action of gravity. Not to speak of difference in the weight of bodies to a diver under water, nor of the effect of a strong magnet held over an iron weight in a scale, we know that weight itself alters in the air, while the matter remains, so far as we are aware, unchanged. Suspend a pound from a spring-balance, carry it up some height in the atmosphere, and the indicator will show a lessened weight. From a sufficiently delicate spring-balance suspend a weight and allow it to remain on the table: if we could read the minute indications, we should find that the weight did not remain the same for a single hour. Of course all this obtains regulation by the law, or mode, or rule of nature—that means the unknown or Divine manner of doing things: which manner is so vastly complicate, so universally varied by incalculable interruptions effecting differences varying from inappreciable to the most startling magnitude, that only an Infinite Being can know either the total unity of law, or the incalculable differences centred therein, so as to affirm the one or explain the other.

The above can be further verified, and in a somewhat easier form :—A man may be seen walking to London, the rate of his speed is calculated, the distance he has to go, and the time is ascertained at which he should arrive. He does arrive at that time, is proved by many witnesses to have maintained one uniform rate of progress, and to have been invariably found in the high road. All is true, so far as the witnesses are concerned; nevertheless, the man, when not observed, deviated several times; yet, his speed and place on the road were always those, at the times stated, which the witnesses verified.

Again:—Physicists are not omnipresent nor omniscient; it is impossible for them to know that law has never for a moment been suspended, and that nature has never been crossed by spontaneous action. They do know, however, that some physical laws are suspended, and others called into action, every time we move our body; laws of matter are interfered with, suspended and elevated by laws of life; and laws of life are crossed, ruled, and enlarged by those of mind. Material phenomena are visible manifestations of invisible underlying Energy; vital phenomena are resultants of unseen Life; mental phenomena are the garment of unseen Mind—or that we call Mind: therefore there has been, is, and will be a continual crossing of things—as by automatic, or by spontaneous action of other things; so that at no time, by any human or finite mind, could the future be rigorously deduced from the preceding state.

The result actually obtained by continued process of thought is: that "all phenomena, even the most elevated, are the effects of a complication which has come out of the simplest elements;" and that as the lesser cannot contain the greater, and as the formation of an atom is a mystery great as the moulding of a planet, the advance from matter to life, from life to intelligence, from intelligence to emotion, is a series of steps in connection with some grand teleological design. Further—as change in uniformity can only have been wrought within by power from without, every progression must have been by means of interference which is proved by the result to have been designed from the beginning; and, therefore, miraculous. Using a familiar illustration we say reverently—the action of God's Spirit sustaining a man is in some analogy with the action of human mind in holding up a hand. Mind dwells in the flesh—not as an attribute, but a ruler; the Most High dwells yet more transcendently in nature.

To say the least, there are scientific reasons which render probable the derivative origin of nature; and certainly it can be proved that "out of common non-luminous matter the whole pomp of stars might have been evolved." It is an arbitrary and unproved hypothesis that God does not act directly in the ordinary as in extraordinary manifestations. There is no power in nature, so far as we are aware, capable of creating new agencies. It is a received axiom of science that no physical power makes its appearance in nature without an equivalent expenditure of some other power. Natural agents are so related as to be mutually convertible, but no new agency is created. Light runs into heat, heat into electricity, electricity into magnetism, magnetism into mechanical force; and mechanical force back again into heat and light—but not so of necessity. The change is never actually the same. The circumstances alter every moment. There is not, and never was, a perpetual motion in nature: for such motion requires a creation of force which science declares nature to be incapable of. The principle of conversion of force, or energy, is not infinite—not flowing ever onward in the uninterrupted rhythm of cause and effect, but always losing by that scattering into infinite space which ensures the passing away of the stars. As there is no perpetual motion, the motions now observed are not from everlasting, nor do they possess eternal continuance as to the future, nor did they originate themselves before their own existence. They came, therefore, into being by operation of that great Unknown Energy which science now admits to be the Cause of all phenomena, and the Giver to matter of all its properties; by the act and will of that Great Cause whose direct operation we call "miraculous;" but the effect and continuance, though not less miraculous, we call "natural."

We will now gather our Thought as into a point:—It is a grand thing to behold a noble creature—man, commenting upon, and making discoveries as to nature and providence; finding rational manifestations which awaken his reason to what it did not—what it could not—understand before. Man is a marvellous exception, specially in mind, from everything else in nature. Man is a miracle. He dissects the brains of dead men and of living monkeys, trying to show "how the wits crept in and the wits they crept out," and discovers a grand series of marvels. There are breaks where he expected continuance, and barriers, seemingly impassable, are leaped over. Whether he observes the grub—the caterpillar—the moth—the fœtus—the child—the man—there are leaps and surprises, changes and advances, marvellous and unexplainable. Sometimes the process is retarded, sometimes accelerated : for example, if the bird is a metamorphosed lizard, are not its limbs a marvellous, even miraculous, modification of the lizard's, and its feathers of the lizard's scales. Again— no two men are alike : the differences existing between individuals, apparently similar, are innumerable. No two animals, no two plants—though even to the careful observer they seem the same—are really the same. No two leaves, nor two crystals, nor two elementary atoms even, are identical : the lines, axes, weight, may correspond ; nor eye, nor balance, nor microscope, discern unlikeness ; yet unlikeness exists. The solid earth, all living on it, the deep sea, the firmament, are never for any two consecutive moments the same. Pervading all this universe, a pulse—a rhythm—is found : every pulse possessing oneness—its own individuality. Hence, the argument for natural uniformity makes that uniformity the platform of variety, extracts unlike from like : this is a miracle. Every scientific man knows, if he knows anything aright, that by no forces—no laws—no processes now known to be in existence, could matter be formed out of nothing ; could force, only capable of pushing on in a straight line, assume curves, circles, spirals, and other more complicate movements ; could the dead give itself life ; could the unconscious endow itself with intelligence. To assume that intelligence and life and motion are essential properties of matter, is to make matter and nature a wonder great as God. Miracles are proved : height, depth, length, breadth—past, present, future— all beings, all existences—are stupendous as a whole, and a miracle in every part.

THOUGHT XII.

THE UNIVERSE A COMPLEMENT OF INTELLECT.

"Supposé qu'il n'y eût pas d'être parfait, comment en aurais je créée? mais avec quels éléments et d'après quel modèle?"—EMILE SAISSET.

THE material universe is a complement of intellect. A remarkable, yet not often used proof is afforded in the fact, that by study of its laws, and finding their order by means of our intellect, we attain the heights of reason and science.

The matter of the world may be roughly divided into two sorts: atoms and molecules which have already rushed together and satisfied their mutual attractions—these are no longer sources of power, as dynamic agents they are passive; atoms and molecules which have not rushed together, so that their mutual attractions remain unsatisfied, and those compounds still possessing unexpended forces—these can produce motion, and are the only remaining sources of power: a small remnant in comparison with the vast powers already expended.

Nature cannot create matter, nor energy, nor motion; neither the inorganic nor the organic; not plant nor animal can create; neither one thing, nor all things together, can add to nature; there is no power in anything to add one cubic to its stature. Nature, viewed mechanically—and Materialism asserts that it must be so viewed—is surely hastening to destruction, is a fire burning itself out. If so, why has it not already burnt out? The past is eternal as the future is eternal: if the past eternity sufficed not for extinction, neither will the future. As the mechanical theory does not create matter, nor energy; and as the world, on mechanical principles, could not have existed during the whole of the eternal past, any more than it can endure an eternal future, the mechanical principle does not adequately explain either the origin or continuance of things.

We anticipate an answer to the above statement— "Yours is an amazing logic. You might just as well ask why a fire was not out because it had all day to burn out in: the reply being—it was not lighted till the afternoon; so the world and all natural events exist in time." The attempted answer concedes that which we contend for: the world does exist in time, is not eternal; consequently, as the mechanical theory proves that the universe is not self-existent, nor self-supporting, it is derivative, it was created; and before the miracle of creation all other miracles are as nothing.

Again—If nature, even now that it is highly organized, has no creative power; and if mental energy, vital force, chemical affinities and antagonisms, atomic and molecular attractions and repulsions, are all reducible to mechanical forces, and these forces are reducible to push in a straight line; how is it that push in a straight line ever managed to attain, of itself, the angles, curves, circles, spirals, and the other yet more complicated motions represented in nature? A thing with straight line as the foundation, essence, and sum total of its being, must be a straight line for ever: no world could be moulded, nor tear be rounded.

Again—If matter, the sixty-four elements known, must be regarded as the offspring of one primal diffused substance, without parts or properties of any kind; and the ancient maxim be true—"Out of nothing, nothing comes;" how did matter become possessed of parts and properties so as to give weight, activities, nature, to that which was natureless, inert, imponderable, and incapable of shape or figure? If nature was always substantially the same, ever flowing onward in the uninterrupted flow of cause and effect; not able to create new matter, nor new force, always hastening to extinction, and incapable of creating new agency; how can it have been invariably the same? It never was the same for any two consecutive moments. We cannot, even in ourselves, be always sure as to which of our actions are voluntary or involuntary, spontaneous or automatic; why should we say of the whole world that no part of it has ever been crossed by Divine spontaneous action; when it must have been so crossed, or it would long since have become extinct?

We will put nature into the witness-box:—

Everywhere, throughout nature, we find formative power. Molecules attract and repel one another, at certain points or poles, and in definite directions. These forms and directions are complex, and the complexity partly explains the differences of crystalline and all other structures. The architecture of a living grain of corn somewhat resembles, but is infinitely more complex than, the architecture of a crystal. The crystal adds to its surface in order to increase in size. The

The Universe a Complement of Intellect. 95

plant, as regards the cells, makes increase within; and forces are active at the root, the stalk, the ear, the full corn in the ear. In the animal the organic can be traced to the inorganic, but the forces are not to be considered as of the same kind: the difference in nature, in complexity, is immeasurable. The architecture of the plant and of the animal exceeds the architecture of the crystal. Blocks of crystal deposit themselves, and we have little pyramids with terrace above terrace from base to apex; the operation seems not wholly mechanical, but as if an invisible population under an unseen master, gave position to the atomic blocks. By more subtle remote formative acts, including chemical vital mental expenditure, are highest organisms constructed.

Of the inner quality or qualities enabling matter thus to attract matter, move, form crystals, effect growth, and manifest intelligence, we know nothing more than the results. The various manifestations are called by different names, but the same energy which pulls an apple from the tree, holds together all worlds, "moulds a planet and rounds a tear." A modification of this power, in connection with energies subtle, vital, and intellectual in effect, constructs the plant and builds the animal, is the source of all our emotions, the means by which we think our thoughts, and enables us to reveal those thoughts and emotions. We endeavour to show the mystery by deepest, furthest-reaching investigation, but within every depth is a greater deep; and by no possible means can the most intellectual of our Divines, or the profoundest Physicist, state where the material ends or the spiritual begins.

Could we see, as Newton thought might sometime

be possible, the ultimate atoms; behold the waves of light æther, know their size, form, and force; trace atom to molecule; find latent in the amorphous drop of water all the marvels of crystalline force; examine the breaking up by the sunbeam of the carbonic acid of the atmosphere within the plant into elements of growth; and the same dynamic power brought differently into display for construction and repair of animal bodies; these outward and inner visible phenomena would be but counters of the intellect—not revealers of the mystery. They would only demonstrate the interdependence and harmony of all things; but we could not detect nor precisely explain the essential difference between volitional and mechanical operation; for the whole world is like a living creature praising God. Atoms and molecules march in tune; more melodious strains awake in crystalline force; the pitch is changed for that symphony in which the trees clap their hands; then come a blending and variety, richer and higher, in cattle of the thousand hills, culminating in the grand oratorio and outpoured praise of men; the whole attuned and made responsive in various harmonies.

Now, as it is certain that water rises not above its own level, and that everything is limited by, and cannot exceed, its own nature, we are unable by any merely mechanical theory to explain the origin or continuance of such a wonderful universe as an organism whose powers, motion, heat, life, intelligence, were latent in the diffused mist, whether of cold or fiery cloud. Complex, various, and opposing motions could not possibly originate by means of a simple straight push. The many substances of different and contrary properties could not be formed by pushing along the same formless diffused thing in a straight line. That one push, centreless, guideless, would impel all matter on and on into new portions of infinitude, leaving traversed regions empty—for ever empty. There is no such godless progression of nothing to something, of shapelessness to the rounded world, of the inorganic to the organic, of life to intelligence. The lesser cannot contain the greater, nor time infold eternity, nor place enwrap infinitude.

We shape the Thought otherwise :—

Let a man observe himself; he feels as well as moves, thinks as well as feels, is morally as well as intellectually conscious. He cannot wholly separate the moral and emotional from the intellectual, the sentient from the mere living, nor the living from the mechanical; thus gradationally he descends to the inorganic. There is no vast chasm anywhere; one and the same power, one and the same principle, are manifest throughout, inextricably interwoven; but differing in the masses and complexity, in the nature and essence of the processes involved.

Now take the other side of this truth :—

Suppose we gather, first-hand from nature, the molecules of the human body—not so as to replace or renew a pre-existent form, but to make a new being. By structural energies we gather the mass with its forces and put them together in the same positions as those occupied by a human body, there being "the self-same forces and distribution of forces, the self-same motions and distribution of motions, would this organized concourse of molecules stand before us as a sentient thinking being?" Science answers—"There seems no valid reason to believe that it would not." Thus we attain to man.

Man is the complement, the symbol, or contains the likeness in his spirit, of the world's intellectual constructive process; seems, himself, however feebly, to represent that Wonderful One by whom, and for whom, the universal process is wrought. Man is able, in a measure, to give his own plan—power—spirit—to that which he forms; and thus obtains an analogy, very feeble, yet true and actual—or there is no human analogy—of Him who organizes, gives life and intelligence to the world.

This world, though it changes continually, is relatively eternal—being created by the Absolutely Eternal. There will be in it, unless the constitution of our mind and all our scientific principles err, unfailing and universal subordination of parts to grand principles of law culminating in some sublime teleology. This enlarged view enables us to see how the notion of Fate arose; and, while it gives consistency to the Scriptural Plan of Redemption, admits and requires that the many worlds of infinitude be in connection and unity with some all-embracing scheme; and yet in every part separately complete. For the maintenance of this grand unity and teleology, there exists that continual intervention and interaction which unite all the links into one grand chain of universal cause and effect. Evidence of the above is afforded by Astronomy. The systems of suns, planets, satellites, comets, meteors; elliptic, parabolic, and other planes of motion; of sun round sun, and centres dominated by other centres; are examples of union, communion and intervention, of the passage of energy, light, heat, motion; which evidence that the universe is sustained, as to the whole and in every part, by all-pervading Wisdom and Might.

The telescope, we are informed, reveals stars in which life, such as we are acquainted with, may have existed; but can now have no place. There are other spheres in which life is affirmed not now to exist, but time may bring it. Life brings new interferences, and the volition of animal life is raised to reason and conscience; these interferences, whether sudden and startling, or gradual with beginning and operation imperceptible, are in no wise marks of weakness, of imperfection in design, of inadequacy; but are means, unfoldings, and displays of that wonderful variety which we discern in distant realms of space, where stars die and new worlds brighten, so that as the old pass away new life brings in its own power, its own beauty.

THOUGHT XIII.

AUTOMATISM.

"Through some awkwardness on my part, I touched a wire leading from the battery, and the discharge went through my body. Life was absolutely blotted out for a very sensible interval, without a trace of pain. In a second or so consciousness returned ... The appearance which my body presented to myself was that of a number of separate pieces. The arms, for example, were detached from the trunk, and seemed suspended in the air."—JOHN TYNDALL.

IT may be deemed necessary, in order to prove the reality of miraculous occurrences, that a sort of spontaneousness be exhibited in nature; by which doing and not doing, rest and motion, life and death, attractions and repulsions, are wrought from within by a power which manifests itself externally; by which emotional, intellectual, and optical suspensions changes and deaths of consciousness, as in the above example of Professor Tyndall, seem akin to the Supernatural.

This we undertake, observing, as we pass on, that there is a great difference between the verification of any one miracle, and a verification of miracles generally. The whole are capable of proof as probable, reasonable, natural, as parts of a great plan; but for verification of any one in particular, it must be seen by ourselves, or certified by adequate testimony. The historical evidential proof of miracles is greater than any that can be given as to the life and actions of Julius Cæsar. The general scientific argument is stronger than the historical, stronger even than that derived from eyesight of any one marvel: for in one, mistake is possible. Moreover, a miracle occurring—say once in every two centuries, like the translation of Elijah, or like the resurrection of Lazarus, or prophecy like the foresight of Isaiah; could possibly be explained by an unknown law of intermittent exercise, which endowed a human being with levitation, the faculty of suspending and restoring consciousness, and endued a few unusual intellects with remarkable power of prevision. Not so with the general argument: that not only renders probable any one miracle, but attains the height of certitude with regard to miracles as a whole, or in general.

Our first thought, as we look at the sky, is—the stars are sprinkled by confusion. The next thought is as to the vastness of space and manifoldness of worlds. Afterwards, by examination and reflection, our reason discovers an arrangement—an intelligible plan, motions and forces which can be calculated, events which may be predicted, harmonious interaction, subordination and compensation, which by means of constant change and variety ensure permanence and comprehensive unity.

That is not all. Mr. J. S. Mill ("Logic," B. 3, c. xxi. § 1) states—There is "no difficulty in conceiving that in some one of the many firmaments into which siderial astronomy now divides the universe, events may succeed one another at random without any fixed law. Nor can anything in our experience, or in our mental nature, constitute a sufficient, or indeed any reason, for believing that this is nowhere the case." He is right: the permanence which we find is not a fated but a reasonable fixity, such as our understanding approves.

Life is, in itself, a marvel; but to be endued with the power of reproduction, for living things to have the faculty of life in themselves, for kind to bring forth after their kind, to have seed in themselves, is a wonderful automatism! There are strange manifestations of it: we find, for example, a spontaneousness by which distant parts are suppressed, or over-developed; bones of animals are lengthened or shortened, strengthened or lightened, straightened or bent, to suit the particular functions and habits of every sensitive creature. So far is this carried that, little by little, a tentative teleology works adaptation to even the least of things surrounding; new species are formed; and sometimes, at a leap, wonderful life and unusual powers enter and manifest themselves.

We might not think much of the luminosity induced in many substances by mechanical or chemical action; nor of those vivid illuminations which disappear so soon as the source ceases to be in the presence of the illuminated object; though sufficiently remarkable. Vessels containing sea-water, crowded with luminous animals, may be so placed that their illuminations put together, and reflected upon different parts of the room, make it appear as if it were on fire. Noctiluca, a flagellata infusorian, many medusæ, and the shell-fish Pholas, and numbers of better known marine things, are remarkable for luminosity. The wonders grow when we come to other organized and living things, and though the mode of producing light is nearly unknown, we are sure that the will of the animal plays a peculiar part—actually calling into existence, using, and controlling for its own purposes, many and various natural powers. The luminosity of the glow-worm and of the fire-fly, and of their bodies even when the head has been removed, and of their ova, is, by automatic kindling of their own lights, a natural marvel which human wisdom cannot explain. We may safely assert that such an automatous use of power within and without; the interference, not constant but continuously intermittent; is not an accident, but a light kindled from the depths of a deeper spontaneity to lead the profoundly rational to new discoveries and cognitions as to nature having life in itself.

The thought may be rendered more definite:—Many invertebrates cast off limbs, and grow new ones, *e.g.*, star-fish, and Brittle Stars in impure water: the casting off is automatic and wilful, according to the case. Birds, when robbed of their eggs, lay again and again that they may ensure a progeny; animals shape their conduct so as to use means for attainment of an end; and that continual, varying, advancing, or retrograding evolution, in which not only the need but the will of animals counts for something; are evidence of interference and intervention. That is, we recognize in nature an unconscious activity of reason—we trace it in crystals, in sensitive plants, in sea-anemones, in the artistic impulses of animals; in history too we recognize the same unconscious activity, the highest embodiment of which in human nature we designate genius. Every little likeness of it, we may count a miniature drawn out by a Master Hand from the inexhaustible fountains of new signs, new beginnings, new revelations, new possibilities.

The magic visions playing in these inner self-revelations of power without and within, of automatism and consciousness, are rightly accounted determining factors in our knowledge of creation: for says Humboldt—"The highest and most important result of the investigation of physical phenomena, is the knowledge of the connection of the forces of nature, the deep sense of their mixed dependence." The plastic, or consummating, or completing principle, makes the universe, in very deed, not chaos but creation—an orderly system—having Mind for the primal original Being and Existence: Mind manifested in the spontaneity of kind after its kind; Mind bringing together all nature in a chain of various links, every one united by indissoluble affinity; Mind evidenced in that continuance of automatism which makes way for itself as out of a dark womb. This rhythm of vitality, of reason, never ceases, though the manifestations are often intermittent. The qualities of this rhythm give the powers, or modulate the powers, of the principal and mother elements whereof all things in this lower world are composed. Its principles frame the arch erected over our heads, so that it is neither loosed nor dissolved; nor can the celestial spheres forget their wonted course, nor by irregular volition turn themselves away. It governs the greater and lesser rulers, and all the lights of heaven; nor do they shine, or rest, or stand by themselves, apart from their fellows. Times and seasons are not blended by confused and disordered mixture; but as the winds breathe, and clouds yield rain, the fruits of the earth are nourished on the breasts of their mother. Thus the automatism, the unconscious reason of nature, is a Heavenly Influence within continually becoming natural, ruling in all things. It is a vast rhythm felt in the ocean swell; heard in all harmonies; seen in every alternation of light, shade, colour; making itself known in poetic swell and cadence; animating the throb of all life; an intelligence moving and acting in all existence.

These roots of visible existence, themselves unseen, are only discoverable by mental digging into the depths whence they issue. How deep these depths, and wellnigh inscrutable the mysteries, we may thus picture:—Imagine the seeds underground conversing as to the manner of their future existence, agreeing that their size and weight will surely be increased, that they shall imbibe more moisture, lay fold on fold by continual swelling. Alike dark and earthly are we when we limit natural or supernatural operations, and are weakly satisfied that our underground cogitations contain all truth. The voice of nature in its continual becoming, the automatism in lower creatures, the texture of our thoughts as to goodness, of our feelings as to righteousness, show traces of a splendid miracle.

We have taken the word "automatism," derived from two Greek works, in the ancient meaning "self-moving." Of late some scientific men have departed from the sense it conveyed to Greek thinkers—a cause of movement and action. Dr. Carpenter says of an automaton, "it means a structure which moves by a mechanism, and which can only move in a certain way." Such a machine—say a watch—is not, in the sense of the Greek word, an automaton at all. Certainly, as applied to Nature and living creatures, it were better to retain the ancient signification, involving either complete or partial freedom of willing and acting; or the absence, more or less, of external agency.

The automatism of nature is somewhat like our own action of habitual co-operation with God: natural yet supernatural. We may call it—"Nature's gift of tongues," and thus translate the speech:—Do not think that God is present only in startling acts, unexpected occurrences, wonderful agencies. He supports the millions with bread, refreshes them with water from the spring, brings the meridian sun, the cloud, the night, makes known His will and law in all things. Be not wilderness-men, unmindful of the miracle of bread because it is a life-long gift; nor count the water less beneficent for flowing through the desert; nor deem that the cloud by day and the fire by night are less than pillars of God on account of their continuance. Let not the frequency of the gift, and the regularity of coming, cause you to forget God—the Giver. You cannot determine the precise kind, manner, and time of Divine action; nor always separate it from that of nature; but whatever nature gives He imparts. He is distinct from nature—controlling it, above nature—ruling it. You, yourselves, are mirrors to reflect His light; are as rays from Him, the Source of light; and, in the purity of moral life and action, are His forces. Present cosmical arrangements are by skilful pre-arrangements, and all remedies exist beforehand by means of providence and government. Miracles are not to correct blunders, are not breakages of laws, are not repairs of imperfect machinery; but are by appointment to give a moral and religious tie; are a free Divine volition and act to meet, restrain, instruct, the otherwise unrestrained freedom of intelligent creatures; and to establish special relations between man and his Maker.

THOUGHT XIV.

SYMBOLS.

"That which is spiritual clothes itself with what is natural, as a man clothes himself with a garment."—ANON.

IF our thought of nature's spontaneity, or of unconscious reason dwelling in every part, awaking to highest sentient and intellectual life in man, be correct; we may probably find likenesses in nature of supernatural things, incipient miracles, hieroglyphical characters which we can read by the light of reason.

Space is not finite: wherever we erect a boundary, we begin again to think of space beyond that boundary; thus, by continual dissolving of limits, we endeavour to form a less inadequate idea of infinitude.

Space is occupied in every part, to which our observation extends, by an all-pervading subtle medium, called æther, through which, or by means of which, acts the energy of gravity welding the universe together: so we enlarge our thought to attain conception of omnipresence.

That all matter may not rush into one mass, the all-piercing attraction is counterbalanced by an all-pervading repulsion. By due adjustment of these opposing forces, we have not only the many starry worlds, but the separate individuality of every atom and molecule in all worlds, with endowment—not of mechanical equality or equilibrium, but of varying and opposing energies, densities, and figures in connection with life, intelligence, and emotion. By persistent, ever-enlarging reflections concerning these marvellous energies we obtain adequate but miniature pictures of omnipotent operations.

By examination of, and reflection concerning all these, let it be repeated, we obtain from space some notion of Infinitude; from æther an idea of Omnipresence; and by government and adjustment of the vast energies at work in the æther, through the infinitude, we gain a thought as to Omnipotence and Omniscience. We appear to be capable of thus using these and other natural symbols by means of inwrought God-consciousness, which is the germ of that sense of responsibility connecting us with the Creator as Author and Giver of eternal life.

Wherever we find a rigid envelope, means of liberty are sure to be at hand; amidst weakness, strength will spring; in the very expectation of death, is some manifestation of life. Iron is strong, water is weak; encircle the water tightly on every side with an inflexible iron shell: the water, in crystallizing, will shiver the iron rim to pieces; it was enclosed as in a tomb, but it comes forth in liberty to run a new race.

Every event in nature taken by itself, apart from all other things, is altogether unnatural; nor can any account or reason be given of it; but all events, viewed together, form that vast arch of which stars are the splendid adornment. In like manner, our Christian Faith, Miracles, Revelations, viewed apart from collateral realities and truths, seem inexplicable and incomprehensible ; but observed as a whole, as explanatory of the world, as indicative of an account to render, as remedial of evil, as manifestations of future blessedness, they enlarge the arch of physical creation into a glorious world-wide cathedral, which they replenish with myriads of beings and existences, every one, in its own way, bringing honour to God ; and every good thing passing from glory to glory.

Take the germs of life. They are all the same, whether of Newton, or his dog Diamond ; of the great whale, or tiny moss. First invisible, always mysterious, and in their early visible stages without structure or characteristic difference. Out of that invisibility, of that nothingness as to difference, of that death, God raises manifold life, marvellous intelligence, sacred emotion, glorious beings, with everlasting splendour for destiny.

Great as are the undetectable conditions which separate the delicate bacterium from the intangible virus of a deadly fever, not less are the Divine potentialities separating the spiritual from a carnal state. That goes on from life to more life, this passes from a life in death to a death in life.

The organic cell integrating the physical qualities of ancestors in new organic product, so that the diseases and madness of men long dead have resurrection in the living, opens hidden recesses in nature ; and shows how a whole eternity of future existence may be marred through evil in our present narrow state and place of being. Two cells are alike to human eye, and to the microscope reveal no inequality, yet one contains the life of John, beloved of Christ; the other of Judas, who became a devil (John vi. 70).

These are letters out of an unknown language—a language yet to be learned. It is evident that the evil must be traced further back than the radical defect in human germ, and that the good possesses an earlier origin than the substance vainly scanned by the microscopic eye. We cannot even think that in Adam was the first germ, or all in all of corruption. Evil is not only the vulgar, malignant thing, darkling in every superstition; but that intensely subtle mischief which seems woven with intensest craft, as by a spirit skilled in wickedness, into every past and present civilization, for the degradation of life in every clime. It fashions devils for the superstitions of India, Japan, and China. It lies at the root of all Hebrew and Christian corruption, hurts the phenomena of nature, and distorts providential events; it makes present and prepares future misery. Good, as manifested in ameliorative advance by Natural Selection; as developed in high art, science, and civilization; as inculcated by Holy Scripture; strives to purify, preserve, and advance life on the Earth. By these means a true spiritual element survives, conveying the conviction of a Great Righteousness—in which we have identity, and consciousness of a Great Divinity in whom we possess unity: Divinity and Righteousness remaining with us through all mental, bodily, and atomic changes, preparing us for immortality, the future harvest of present sowing. These loftier prospects, whether an inherent part or addition to the human constitution, can only be realized by means of a natural and a supernatural miracle: the new birth—by which we live a new life while we live in the old flesh; and the resurrection—by which we find a new life in a spiritual nature, and ascend by ethereal pathway to spiritual spheres.

Those who believe in the development of human language and intellect from brute cries and instinct; ought not to be slowest in discerning that the miracles of speech, recorded in Holy Scripture, were lesser, though quicker marvels. Even if speech is an orderly development from brute cries, while the language and wisdom imparted in Scripture to irrational and speechless creatures were abnormal—an interruption to the existing order of things; it still follows that the difference, put it which way you will, was not in the marvel itself, but in acceleration of the natural and physical process by which it was wrought; and this is a small matter. Of course, it is possible that the miracles were effected in the human consciousness, and not in the animals' organs—that the marvels were subjective, not objective; but it is better to adopt the miracles in all their fulness. Indeed, the wonderment is wellnigh removed by the fact that not the creatures nearest and likest men are gifted with language. Those whose organs, as of the parrot, place them far away, whose capacity science designates incapacity, do sometimes obtain special and startling employment. Marvels are only like common natural events when, standing alone, they seem incredible. Natural events obtain reasonable explanation as parts of a great system; and the miraculous are verified so soon as identified with a process issuing in preternatural benefits. Physical science, moreover, reveals a strange fact, that there is nothing in the organs of the serpent and of the ass that renders them absolutely incapable of producing speech intelligible as that of the parrot; which is not intellectual as to meaning, and of metallic sound somewhat resembling the phonograph; nor can science affirm, as a physical certainty, that there are no evil existences capable of entering, elevating, and directing, or of destroying animal organisms. In a world full of startling and unimagined forms of life, activity, and of energies not yet half known; there are marvels of subjectiveness and miracles of objectiveness; and by either or by both of these the prodigies of Eden, the sights of seers, the inspiration of prophets, the acts of heroes, may be in part illustrated but not explained.

As for the three great characteristic natural history provinces, New Zealand, Australia and South America, in every one of them the present state of things was foreshadowed in the past. There was the same kind of country; but, sometimes, larger, more fertile, moister. The extinct and the living, thus resembling one another, show a deep meaning in nature, and that the same general shape of animal was represented in the same province throughout vast periods of time. This cannot be by accident, everything in the Earth is by law, and this law or rule produced all changes in the world's history, and in the distant past common ancestry. It is quite time that scientific men tell us plainly—" This green flowery rock-built earth, the trees, the mountains, the rivers, many-sounding seas; that deep sea of azure which swims overhead; the winds sweeping through it, the black cloud fashioning itself together, now pouring out fire, now hail and rain; all these are, aye what? We do not know. At bottom can never know at all. They

Symbols. 113

are, after every effort of our science, wonderful! magical! inscrutable! to whomsoever thinks about them. It is by not thinking that we cease to wonder."

We account it high genius and truth in the poet who through every star, through every blade of grass, makes visible the glory of God; and we reckon it a proof of artistic nature to behold a beauty divine in everything. There is more truthfulness, higher genius, deeper poetry, in devout men; who open in every object a window through which to behold Infinitude; and who live resolutely in the whole, the beautiful, the good. They know that there are capacities, and influences mightier than those which eclipse the sun, than those which roll the river St. Lawrence over the falls of Niagara, therefore, these men pray. Pray for a blessing on their undertakings; that every work may be begun, continued, and ended in God; that the rain-drop in the sky, the beam from the sun, adversity and prosperity, life and death; that the law within the law, in every direction, degree, and exigence of nature; may be recognized by their loving faithful spirit as under His guidance whose Love and Wisdom and Power are Infinite.

We will now work a wonder as symbol of a miracle:—

Take a piece of clean glass, and pour over it a little water in which a crystal has been dissolved. By means of a microscope and a lamp, throw an image of the plate of glass upon a screen. The beam of the lamp illuminates the glass, heats it, causes evaporation. When the solution has become "super-saturated," splendid branches of crystal shoot out over the screen, and will cover a dozen square feet of the surface with beautiful forms. With another solution you obtain crystalline spears, other spears feather them right and left; and from various nuclei in the field of view spears shoot with magical rapidity in all directions.

In this small experiment we have used powers which are capable of rolling the river of St. Lawrence up the Falls of Niagara. Intelligence knows how to draw out the marvellous structural energy which lay latent in the solution, and brought it into action by withdrawal of opposing forces. Who shall set limits to the time, the manner, the place, chosen by Higher Intelligence for display of greater marvels?

The little and simple things of life can be clothed by our thought and by our science with beautiful and sublime garments. The development of mystery, and the glorious products of thought and art, are somewhat akin to the ameliorative process that is being wrought in the earth. The mental process, working on and in connection with successive stages of the Earth's development, not only industrially cultivates terrestrial fields—bringing forth stores of art and physical science; but carries on at the same time inner processes concerning vital intellectual and emotional consciousness—which give other and varied effectiveness; so that operations which seemed purely physical, are made to enter man's emotional and moral consciousness, opening into inner worlds of life and beauty. The symbol may be used, by those possessing eyesight and insight, as a sort of shining in the glass of our mind concerning the mysterious brooding of the Divine Spirit in giving birth to worlds. For, indeed, these mental processes remind us of certain crystals—say of

Symbols. 115

fluor-spar, which lie darkly for ages in the earth—and within them a potency of light is locked. Bring these crystals from the depth, warm them, and an outflow of light begins.

There is no rock-barrier between the natural and supernatural. If the Finger of God touch the trigger, marvellous things are done: done softly, done blessedly, done without observation; yet they hold back the wind, send rain, bring prosperity, renewal of life; and, sometimes, so grandly that nations are amazed.

A few men assert that there are rock-barriers—" In nature and from nature, by science and by reason, we neither have, nor can possibly have, any evidence of a Deity working miracles; for that we must go out of nature and beyond reason." By a little change in this assertion, you will see that the very opposite is the truth:—In nature and from nature, by science and by reason, we have—nor can we possibly have other evidence of a Deity working miracles: for we cannot go out of nature, nor beyond reason.

The same author states—"The literal sense of *physical events* impossible to science cannot be essential to spiritual truth . . . . . . the philosopher denies the credibility of alleged events professedly in their nature at variance with all physical analogy." If this philosopher had waited for the lame messenger, he would have spoken more wisely and thus—" The literal sense of physical events, which seem impossible to science by use of ordinary natural means, is essentially a proof of spiritual truth when Divinely wrought by extraordinary means . . . . . . The philosopher can only accept the credibility of alleged events—professedly at variance with all physical analogy—when those events are Divine works wrought to give Divine sanction to spiritual teaching.

Take one more statement, the substance was given long ago by Spinoza :—" If anything happened in nature at large repugnant to its universal laws, this would be equally repugnant to the decrees and intelligence of God." Really, it is very plain, these men, who would carry on the world wholly apart from the Owner and the Maker, are out of their depth. They must mean— "If anything happened in nature at large repugnant to its universal laws; this event, as it could be wrought by Divine Power only, must be regarded as in accordance with, and for effectuation of, a higher policy than nature's ordinary work is able to effect."

Every one may detect for himself mysterious action surrounding and penetrating all things: action in no wise explainable, a depth of unfathomableness in the commonest events. Take example—Between our mind and the outer world are interposed the bodily nerves; which translate, or cause to be translated, impressions from the outer world into facts of consciousness and thought. These facts of consciousness and thought are translated into physical reality by action of our bodies on the outer world. Science cannot explain this. The transition from the physical to the emotional and intellectual, and from the emotional and intellectual to the physical, is incomprehensible; even as is the mysterious action described in Holy Writ—" The Spirit of God moved upon the face of the waters."

We can so magnify, diminish, qualify, and combine experiences, as to render them fit for purposes alto-

Symbols. 117

gether new. Knowledge, in the mind of a thinker, is much more than the sum total of many separate parts. A thoughtful man, acquainted with a fact, connects it with another: he knows then the aspect of each, that is two; then that of either to either, which makes at least four; then the resultants in relation, whether of antagonism or agreement, are at least sixteen in the first operation. These mental energies, not of imagination only, but of reason's highest operation, are forgotten by those who narrow the mind to a mere tabulation of co-existences and sequences.

Take an experiment as to sound :—

We tune two tuning-forks, so far as we can, absolutely alike. They vibrate with the same rapidity and evoke the same musical note; you scarcely hear it; but mount them on a resonant stand, and they sing aloud. Stop one of the forks, and throw the other into yet stronger vibration; bring it near the silent fork, but not into contact. After four or five seconds, stop the vibrating fork. What then? The second has taken up the vibrations, and continues them on its own account. When they are stilled, dismount one fork and throw it into strong vibration, but at a distance you cannot hear it. Now bring the dismounted fork close to but not in contact with the silent mounted one, and out of the silence arises a mellow sound.

We are informed that, by another experiment, a very distinct note can be made to vibrate from a tuning-fork near to the operator; the resonant one being far off and not heard.

These acoustical experiments illustrate our mental principle. Latent complex capacities are made active, new character in the thing is a symbol of the new birth; new life in man, and potentialities existing everywhere, only require release to be brought into action. The physical world responds to our mental, moral, and emotional nature, and our nature is moved by its activities; even an angel, if we are to hear his voice, must excite physical vibrations. Suppose that it was not so always, that sometimes the inner ear alone was addressed, and vision vouchsafed to the inner eye only: would the angels' song on Christmas-Eve, the vision and sound of the Lord in Eden, the glorious spectacle on the mount of Transfiguration, be less wonderful? Does the wonder cease by translation into a more marvellous sphere, and by being made more difficult of understanding? certainly not. Outer symbols of inner truths, physical forms of spiritual figures, are as the body of truth. When we awake sound from stillness, give tongue to the voiceless air, and mingle the strains in harmony to delight the inner and outer man; we possess analogues of sweet associations of sacred sorrow with spiritual pleasure; of confession as to sin evoking a response that true righteousness is ours; of tremors as to judgment quickening movements of holiness within the soul, translating darkness into light, and enabling us to walk evermore as God's dear children.

All this essentially is miraculous: it is the mingling of the human with the divine; and yet, how true and natural it is every man, who will, may verify for himself. If any one say—"It is not marvellous in the sense that deniers of miracle require;" we reply—It is admitted by the greatest physicists that all the material phenomena of nature are manifestations of the Unknown

Power, and inexplicable and transcendental; it follows that aspirations as to truth, desires after purity, the struggle for perfect life, being spiritual or mental phenomena, must also spring from the Unknown Power; and are a manifestation, or revealing in earthen vessels, of that Truth, that Purity, that Perfection, held by Christians to be Divine.

THOUGHT XV.

GROUPING OF MIRACLES.

"Per angusta itur ad augusta."

"... What if all animated natures
Be but organic harps, diversely framed,
That tremble into life as o'er them sweeps
...... Our Intellectual Breeze."

WE scale heaven by means of astronomic ladder and pass from world to world. We divine the history of our earth, and intellectually present ourselves at its origination. We retrace the past, discern the present, foresee the future. All changes are but continuances in another form, and our continuance will not be as that of the bubble which bursts, or as dissolution of moss and lichen into gases, but that change which enables us to gather the gracious flowers of hope, and enjoy the fruit of every holy thought and work: this we know because responsibility involves true personality and real individuality for preservation and continuance of identity.

Whatever may be the real texture of matter, the true substance of mind, or the actual nature of life, there will, when our change comes, be that continuance of our essential selves which the scientific doctrine of continuity requires: for nothing can be annihilated—God does not unmake His own works.

Grouping of Miracles.

Passing by the Miracles of Creation, and only considering miracles as in connection with our continuance as responsible beings, we find that they group about individuals who are made links between God and a people; and that, afterwards, they surround individuals who become the means of knitting all people to the Lord.

The first group of miracles for the guidance, maintenance, and correction of individuals and of Israel, that there may be a peculiar people to witness of Divine Existence and Providence, presents no very great difficulty to a really scientific mind. The fact may be shown by an easy process of thought.

One grand system of life and intelligence occupies the world. Every living creature proceeds from a germ which has power to build up the organism with all its members and faculties. There is no great difference between the process by which is born the wild ass's colt, and that by which man is brought forth. The advance from low to high degree is by an immense number of grades, contemporary or successive, from the undifferentiated particle to the sublime human organism. The plant grows from a germ, first in the dark, then through sunshine and rain, producing stem, leaves, flowers, and fruit. From zoophytic life up to the mammalia is another vast ascending scale; not only in bodily perfection, but in animating principle—whatever that may be—lifting up dull sluggish automatism, hovering on border of the insensate, to the speechless reason of the elephant and dog; thence to human intellect and language. To every seed, to every kind, belongs its own powers of growth, or of automatism, or of sensation, or of sensibility, or of all of them; in the ranks from lowest dulness to the full splendour of intelligence. Throughout all this range and curious variety, from the glimmer of the glow-worm to the genius that blazes in the human countenance, there is that unity of power and plan which shows that the whole comes from one and the same universal and eternal source.

The great organic and intellectual advance does not seem to be by inherent essential power of the constituent elements; for, in that case, as the elements are alike, or nearly so, in all organisms, the advance would be in all or none. We find that actually things which are alike in the whole and every part, become utterly unlike both in inner and outer parts. We say it is by a law which we do not understand, but it is more than that: the natural process is essentially miraculous; for as nature does not create, it cannot, of itself, constitute differences where no ground exists for their superstructure. The modifications are sometimes by imperceptible growth, sometimes are very sudden, sometimes are most surprising. An embryo of little more than a quarter of an inch in length is discerned to be that of a mole: the metamorphoses have been run through at a great rate. Take a caterpillar: it does nothing but eat, it lives to eat; it becomes a chrysalis, and is then in a trance without motion; but such internal and external change is wrought that when the butterfly comes forth—neither eating nor drinking—it may fairly be called of another genus. Its shape so different, its nature so changed, its life so altered, its habits so various, that vast leaps have been made, great organic modifications wrought, as were an infinite book of secrets condensed into one page of insect life. With leaps equally surprising, nature passes over whole orders in embryonic development of mammalia to produce the permanent type. By means of other leaps, not less surprising, some of the highest animals attain a special cleverness answering, in some lower degree, to the genius of peculiarly gifted men. These physical marvels attending the progress and change of organisms, and their synthesis into the two kingdoms—animal and vegetable—with their psychological varieties and degrees of advance, are analogies of, and render credible, those physical, mental, and moral marvels which constituted and continued the training of the Abrahamic family—so that it might become a nation; and the nation attain high degree as the world's regenerator. If in the change of a poor grub's life and nature, there are physical and psychological marvels which science cannot account for and hardly tabulate; if everywhere we discern leaps and surprises which no physicist can explain; are we to refuse credence to those well attested marvels which produce, accompany, and develop the new life unto which Abraham's children were called? The reply must be unhesitating and decisive—certainly not.

By accurate mental process, we also blend the second group of miracles into the world's unity. This group surrounds Christ and the Apostles. As wrought by Him, or for Him, they attest His nature, His office, His work. They denote the physical changes which are to be wrought in the world, the victory to be gained over sin and death, and the growth of righteousness.

The chain of evidence which linked our science and faith as to the first group, also binds our understanding to the miracles of Christ and the Apostles: but as in using a varied process we gain additional evidence and strength we will think in another form :—

Every New Testament miracle regards both present and future time : is effectual for physical help, for moral training, for doctrinal teaching. We need but think of the miracles as to bread in order to see a meaning that concerns the life of the world. The wine at Cana's marriage feast is prophetic of better drink at a higher marriage and spiritual banquet. Marvels on the water, in the wilderness, in the city ; miracles of healing and resurrection ; are tokens of a great power which coming into the world binds men to God and His Christ with other and more than natural ties. They are all, so to speak, object lessons concerning the actual abiding energizing presence of God in the world ; and, especially, of God in Christ ; even as we know—

> " That the base world, now Christ hath died,
> Ennobled is and glorified."—KEBLE.

Laying aside all recondite reasoning, lest we make that seem natural which is intensely supernatural ; and fearing to enter the depths into which we would not lead any but the faithful ; we lay our hand on a familiar example—the Bee. In a hive, say of 30,000, are the queen, the drones, the workers. The queen—with sensations, perceptions, capacities in common with her subjects—has those qualities which incite and enable her to lead forth her subjects in migrations and swarmings. The drones—possessed with a love of home—are apparently idle. Their sisters—the workers—are endowed with the love of perpetual labour and gifted with mechanical skill. The various physical and psychological varieties, in one and the same kind of insect, constitute a world of wonders. In tiny form, we find a ganglionic apparatus and instincts so varied and marvellous that all the efforts of a hundred naturalists fail to explain; a wonderful series of physical breaks, leaps, surprises; and endless psychological marvels. In every working bee are the senses of sight, hearing, taste, feeling, smell; the love of work, and love of honey. Every one is impelled to wander over fields, and to search for flowers. Every one possesses skill to find, and will to carry off, the three sorts of material needed in the hive. They all remember or find the way home again, however distant, taking the nearest line thereto. They elaborate wax, build cells, deposit honey, feed the children of their queen. The intelligence or instinct guiding them assumes mathematical form in building hexagons, economical form in use of material, martial form in governing the action of their sting, loyal form in obedience to their queen, and social form in binding the workers—the aristocrats—the royalty—into one people or nation. Are these preparations, arrangements, complications, for the safety and government of a little people; more easy to explain, more natural, less marvellous, than the preparations—arrangements—complications which surround the Redemption of the world? They are not. We speak reverently: as the lilies of the field are so clothed by the Almighty, that Solomon in all his glory was not arrayed like one of them; as there is expended so marvellous a store of wisdom, of goodness, of might, in the welfare of an insect; these tiny facts are a window through which we behold Infinity: and render credible, aye certain, that God who cares more for us, has done things equally good for the continuance of our being, and for the exaltation of our destiny.

The statement has been made that our Lord in His teaching, and that the Apostles in their preaching and writing, did not lay much stress upon miracles.

The statement is erroneous. Our Lord said that the Jews would be justified in their refusal to accept Him, had He not done among them works which no other man did (John xv. 24). St. Paul states plainly that the whole truth of Christianity rests on the miracle of Christ's resurrection, and that Christ's resurrection is proof of the general resurrection (1 Cor. xv. 12-17). St. Peter asserts the ascension of Christ, and the second advent of Christ (1 Peter iii. 22; v. 4); the miracle of divine inspiration and prophecy, the destruction of Sodom and Gomorrha, and the renewal of the world (2 Peter i. 21; ii. 6; iii. 10-13). St. James declares that the coming of the Lord draweth nigh, and that prayers are miraculously answered (James v. 7, 14-18). The whole argument and all the facts of the Epistle to the Hebrews are based on the miraculous. St. Jude, in his small epistle, mentions at least eight miracles (*see* verses 5, 6, 7, 9, 11, 14). St. John states that our Lord's miracles were too numerous for relation (John xxi. 25). It is high time for all men to know this; and that all Scripture and the whole of Nature are based on miracle and confirmed by miracle; and is it not a miracle that He whose sceptre was a reed, whose diadem was a crown of thorns, and whose throne was a cross, is filling the world with his doctrine, and winning all men to his sway?

THOUGHT XVI.

SPIRITUAL INSIGHT.

"He that hath God's Word can hear His silence."

STEP by step, the moral, intellectual, and spiritual realms, with all the complex action of human life, are being added to the domain of inductive science. Our best thinkers not only carry the exactitude of physical law into the mental world, but use the elasticity of spiritual rule for wiser interpretation of the material universe. We, thereby, obtain more freedom and more accuracy; our knowledge is corrected and enlarged concerning both sides of life.

Materialists and Secularists who say—"You cannot live for both worlds, because you do not know both, you know but one"—are convicted of folly by the fact that they, themselves, cannot live for one only: an attempted one-sided life is always a miserable failure, ending in moral death to the individual, and in extinction of the nation.

The union of moral welfare with material well-being, of spiritual energy with physical activity, so knits together the spiritual and physical that we cannot allow miracles in one realm and deny them in the other; nor exclude them from this while they have free course in that. A miracle, whatever inaccurate men say, must be regarded on both sides. On one side, reason investigates it as a matter to be solved, if possible, by physical science; and if not soluble, reason waits expectant and watchful. On the other side, reason investigates morally, spiritually, sacredly; and it is only when miraculous narratives are approved by reason that they become articles of faith. This scientific conviction is attained by spiritual insight.

We do not go out of nature and beyond reason to prove miracles, any more than we depart from physics in mentally considering material effects. No physical fact is absolutely unique; nor does our limited knowledge allow us fully to verify it; it is dependent upon ten thousand other facts which are absolutely unknown. No Miracle stands apart by itself—unrelated, uncaused as to origin, or working, or effect. Physical science, being incompetent to explain fully any natural event, calls for faith in the unseen and unknown. Spiritual science not merging miracles in doctrines supernaturally enforced, nor hiding them within pale of the Sanctuary, carries them forth into the physical field; and engaging in the open conflict of faith against unfaith, of reason against unreason, with two-fold evidence enforces conviction.

Materialists say—"The invariable operation of a series of eternally impressed consequences, following in some necessary chain of orderly causation, is read in all history, life, and spirit." The science of Spiritual Insight being wider, more accurate, further sighted, reveals the inadequacy of that statement:

shows that physical antecedents and sequences are not always the same; but are capable of, and receive infinite variety and modification by law within law which is not yet tabulated. Spiritual science appeals to all law, Divine and human; to all experience, to all consciousness, to all history. It makes known the fact that physical strength and material well-being are accompaniments and consequences of moral purity and intelligent activity: that purity, whether moral or physical, cannot be lasting in an individual, or permanent in a nation, separated from the sacred reverence arising from a desire to be well-pleasing unto God.

Opponents of miracles speak of Moses' large serpent and the small ones of Jannes and Jambres; of great wonders by true prophets, and of lesser wonders by false prophets; of the transcendent works of Christ, and of operations by the Prince of Darkness; not in acceptance of any, but in utter denial of all. Inquiring for the quantitative difference, they assert all are true or none; if all are not demonstrative of goodness, Christ is none the better for doing works such as no other man was able to perform.

We reply—the difficulty is not greater than that which accompanies gifts and uses of other powers. Men may be as angels of goodness, or as demons of darkness, every endowment can be rightly used, or utterly perverted; be brought to nothing, or be marvellously exalted. Goodness and badness depend upon the inward motive: the inner perfection of Christ is outwardly manifested and proved by works of purity and might in alliance with the Supreme. The moral depravity of the Evil One, and of all like him, is evidenced by passing into enormity and godlessness. No shadow of fiction is here, no empty abstraction; and, as *ex nihilo nihil fit*, the palpable reality is visible proof of the exciting cause. We present no solution of evil, it was not an essential part of the Divine Scheme; it is not an essential in anything, and is by all means to be driven away. The effects, as to our own world, were foreseen ere its foundation and provision made for pardon and cure in Christ. It came in, we conceive, by the abused freedom of an intelligent creature or creatures; it is overruled so as to be unto us a peculiar means of discipline, and the procuring cause of a specially wonderful plan for our amelioration, and the taking away of all evil from faithful men by the Son of God.

Physical evil is a growth out of, and in some respects the embodiment of, spiritual evil; and is material antagonism to God, corresponding with the inner spiritual resistance of human or satanic will to the Divine Will. Both difficulties are insoluble by mere physics; nor is our present sight, even aided by spiritual optics, sufficiently far-seeing and comprehensive to bring the whole within view. The only unerring attainable physical conclusion is—our world is not perfect; in some way or other, it and all it contains have been marred. This marring renders the creation, as subject to ordinary laws, incapable of manifesting and maintaining a perfectly true and fully convincing view of Divinity. Nature and its laws are not everywhere beneficial: indeed "the whole creation groaneth and travaileth in pain" (Rom. viii. 22).

Spiritual insight carries our view somewhat further. If God is God—a real God; not merely the contriver of a physical organization, but of an organism suitable to the wants of beings capable of moral responsibility; He must be regarded as capable of voluntary action. Not only so, as our own personality cannot spring from impersonality—otherwise something can come from nothing—God must be Personal. A Personal God acting by Volition, is more than a Force; He is a moral being with will and power of action. Locke says—"It is as certain that there is a God as that the opposite angles made by the intersection of two straight lines are equal." Devout men know this.

We will now, as it were, experiment a little. The optic nerve passing from the brain to the back of the eyeball spreads out there to form the retina, a web of cells, fibres and filaments, to receive the images of external objects. This nerve is limited to apprehension of the phenomena of radiation; not making all the rays visible, which are infinite in variety, only those forming the spectrum. These rays pass through space by a medium invisible, and beyond the reach of any of our senses. Space, though traversed by rays from all suns and stars, is itself unseen; but everywhere sky particles are strewn through the atmosphere, and often they swathe the mountain-peaks, spread a delicate gauze over slopes of pine, and so mingle heaven and earth that we are as men already with firm footing on the promised land.

Now take an experimental tube, fill it with atmospheric air and nitrite of amyl vapour. The tube seems quite empty, the air and vapour are both invisible. Let an electric beam play upon the mixture, slightly converging the beam to a focus in the middle of the tube. The tube remains dark for a moment, then suddenly the darkness is banished by a luminous white cloud pierced by the beam, and a shower of liquid particles flashes forth like a solid luminous spear. Change the scene and experiment. Ascend a hill when the sun is near setting and a few scattered neutral-tint clouds float in the air but fail to catch the dying light. Use a Nicol prism to look at them through the track of the solar beams, turn the prism ninety degrees round its axis: at once the sky's brightness is restored, and the clouds are dark in contrast with it. Take other positions of the prism, and the light of the sky is so nearly quenched that the clouds are white in the darkness. These simple experiments, by means of which the sky seems so changed—a change wrought by means which are put in operation by the mind and will of man, may be fairly deemed typical of apparent and real changes wrought in us, and wrought in nature, by agencies put in operation by the Will of God.

By other experiments, all the colours of the solar spectrum are extracted from dark rays. In darkness men can prepare heat sufficient to set London on fire. Platinum is made red hot by means of heat that the optic nerve is utterly unconscious of. Out of invisible vapour can be formed a deeper, purer blue than that seen in Italian sky. After due preparation, the scientific man stands at a distance of twenty feet from a jet of gas, and, at command, the flame emits a melodious note, and continues a song for hours, to be heard by a thousand people. These are natural wonders, a light-giving insight: so that when we read in Holy Writ that God made the Bush to shine as were it His pavilion; gave light in the land of Goshen; turned

His face in dark cloud against the Egyptians; assured brightness to Israel; sent fire to consume Fifties of the ungodly; and radiated blessed light from the form and robes of Jesus—causing Apostles to wonder; we thank Him for these displays of goodness and might: and thank Him for the gift of reason and science, as a means whereby we obtain physical illustrations to aid our spiritual discernment of Divine realities.

These witnesses and testimonials as to miraculous things can only be known by the unthinking many in general and superficially. Like all matters of high science, they are to be verified by a chosen few; and, in this science, the learners are taught of God. They know that miracles are sparks, kindled by Omnipotence, to brighten on the wheel of nature; that varieties are the sport of Wisdom to diversify the level of life. It is well to be glad of these lights which God throws on creation to illuminate the great picture of His own painting. They are a touch of nature by Divinity; they are as a re-creation in creation, making nature itself affect the Supernatural. It is a way not approved by the sinful disputers in our world, but it gives wisdom to the minds of men, and drops happiness as honey into the mouths of babes.

THOUGHT XVII.

ACTION OF SPIRIT ON MATTER.

"Two principles of all existence, the active and the passive: the passive, which is but the characterless stuff of the world; the active, which is the Reason that pervades it, even God."—DIOG. LAERT. vii. i. 134.

"We view and embrace some end abstractedly from means. Then we create means, labour for, and finally obtain, the end by the physical effects of instrumental causes."

MEN, taught by nature and reason, hold the physical in subordination to the moral and spiritual. Science aims at controlling and elevating the laws of matter by those of mind. Notwithstanding, we meet with a difficulty: it is said—"The analogy of nature does not furnish any instance of mental feeling causally influencing an object or an event with which it has no physical connection."

The assertion, like most materialistic dogmas, is only superficially scientific. Put it in another form by alteration of two words—"The analogy of nature does not furnish any instance of physical power causally influencing an object or an event with which it has no physical connection." How then do physicists account for the passage of light, heat, electricity, magnetism, gravity through space? By supposing—for no actual proof exists—that there is a medium, a sort of ethereal link, or way, by which matter acts through space upon other distant and diverse matter. Let us, then, suppose, in our case, as physicists do in theirs, that there is a medium which, partaking both of matter and spirit, is that through which Spirit acts in ruling the world.

If materialists will not concede the probability that such a medium exists, we must try to do without the concession, and reason thus:—Our thought seems to possess unbounded freedom in the faculty of compounding, transposing, augmenting, diminishing, the materials gathered by our senses; but we cannot create thought any more than we can create matter. It follows from this, that however little the beginning, or gradual the growth, there is no power in an unthinking substance to begin to think, or to create an idea. Our opponents may take their choice—"Thought is a property of matter," or "Thought is an attribute of some spiritual substance which we call mind." In either case, matter did not always think; and, as there is no known or knowable link between matter and spirit, intelligence did begin, some time or other, to act upon matter with which it had no physical connection.

View it in another way:—

Thought, idea, belief, sentiment, which are acts, emotions, or states of the mind—exist within us by means of excitement from without; and their nature is determined by the situation, or condition, in which the mind is placed at any particular juncture by presentation of objects to the senses and memory. We can make fictions, but only by putting reals into contrariety with our experience; feign centaurs and mermaids by joining the head of a man to the body of a horse, or the head and body of a woman to the tail of a fish. These fictions never attain, in the mind of a sane person, to the reality of belief. Belief is that something in us which separates the ideas of the judgment from fictions of the imagination; gives them weight and value, and constitutes them the ruling principles of our conduct; so that the figment of an enchanted castle possesses not the hold, or reality in us, which is obtained by existing things. The process of belief being in accordance with, or by a kind of pre-established harmony between, the course of nature and the succession of our ideas; so that we are able to adjust means to end, and conjoin knowledge to the use of our natural powers—whether to do good, or to effect evil. Belief, therefore—or trust in the reality of things—becomes or is a kind of internal energy by which we use internal reflection to act on and through the organs of our body, or to direct the faculties of our mind. It seems to be a medium whereby externals excite volition of the spiritual substance, called "soul," which soul or mind controls the material substance of our body. We hereby acquire conviction and knowledge as to the fact that matter acts upon intelligence in forming conviction, and intelligence acts upon matter when putting conviction into use or work; but as to the essential nature of the operation we do not know anything.

Spirit may communicate directly with matter, or there may be many and different media, who knows? The imponderables, heat, light, electricity, magnetism, gravity, communicate with one another and with other things; what is the medium? or are there more than one? Is æther the only? or may there be other—both inner and outer? By what medium is the instinct of animals imparted; and so imparted that not only every species has its own nature, but every individual its own character? The disposition of one fly is not the disposition of another, nor the magnanimity of one mouse the measure of another's courage. We do not know what physical connection there is between the serpent's fascination and the victim's impulse toward the object of dread. The protean nature of the grub, the chrysalis, the butterfly, is not fully explained; nor do we find any sufficient account of the mental action on and in our own frame. Matter, at a distance, does act upon us; and our mind, through distance, acts upon matter; otherwise, why do we close our eyes to aim the better? Why do we even shut our ear against reason, that we may have more abundant compensation in faith? When the imagination, in witty mood with laborious pencil, transfigures or represents the shapes, proportions, and distances of persons and places; it is by an operation of that we call spirit in connection with what we call matter, and of what we call matter with that we call spirit; and the connection and the mingling are that enigma of life, which we do well devoutly to study, for vintage of the natural, and for gleaning of the spiritual. Piercings of matter by these gleams of thought testify of an inward affinity borne by all nature to the spirit-world.

There is no possible knowledge of the world, except in reference to our minds. Solidity, extension, space, fundamental properties of the material world, respond to certain movements of our bodies; and exist in our minds as sentiments of force, as visual and tactile impressions. The conclusion at which Mr. Bain seems to arrive is—The feeling and the felt are not two terms, but two complementary parts of the same whole. If we accept this, it follows that nature is bound together into one whole; that physical phenomena, natural and mental and moral emotions, are transformations of motion; and that every phenomenon is instinct with the all-pervading and unknown energy.

This material chain of nervous actions, of visible and invisible links, of visible and invisible messages, answers to the fact that every mental action presents two faces; an effect produced by the mind, and an effect produced by the mind joined with the body. Now it is impossible to think of mind by itself without placing ourselves, in conception, outside the world of space; on the other hand, all ordinary unions of mind and body are presented to us under the form of a connection in space; the correct expression of the passage towards one another, is a change of condition, and their union is the continuous line of conscious life. How spirit and matter, essentially distinct, having nothing in common, do, nevertheless, act upon one another is a mystery; but certainly a fact.

It is no explanation to say, as some do—"Mind is the physical aspect of life, that is the sum total of the whole sensitive organism, as life is the sum total of the whole vital organism;" for how can the union in a sum total of such dissimilar things be explained by a word meaning but one sort of them? We may say, with approximate correctness—consciousness has its synthe-

Action of Spirit on Matter. 139

sis in the continuity of vital conditions, and mind has its synthesis in the series of states of consciousness; but how to explain the continuity, or even to state it, no man findeth.

The truth arrived at by the above reasoning is—The means or links of connection between mind and matter cannot be found or known by any human understanding; therefore, the statement, "that mind, or mental feeling, cannot causally influence an object with which it is not physically connected," is *ultra vires*, wholly incapable of proof.

Now reverse the process of thought.

Our will finds itself in action; we train a dog, and he fetches a bird for us. In what manner our will influences his, and the canine will moves the canine body, is a mystery great and unexplainable as the action of a prophet's mind—if there was any action—by which the soul of the dead child returned to its bodily dwelling. Between the overt act of corporeal movement, of which we are cognizant, and the internal act of mental determination, of which we are also cognizant, there intervenes a numerous series of intermediate agencies of which we have no knowledge; and, consequently, we possess no consciousness of any causal connection between the extreme links of the chain—the will to move and the object moved.

Our ignorance does not, however, hinder or disprove the fact that both low and high mental states may and do produce events with which they seem to have no physical connection. There is, naming only a few examples: there is a will-power in man, an automatism in the lower animals and in nature, by which the biologized subject acts more or less unconsciously; by which the brute is moved by instinct and against instinct, and by which will-force combines at our pleasure with physical force. Take a stone in your hand, if you simply let it go it will fall in a straight line towards the earth's centre; but you can, before it goes, predict a curve and make it describe that curve ere it reaches the ground. By command of your will-force over physical force you so adjust natural things as to obtain the desired result. Men may talk to you about "eternal conservations, invariabilities, and indestructibilities;" but you can confute them and spoil all their theories, within a very wide sphere, whenever you please. You can predict what no other prophet or philosopher is able to foretell, and you can accomplish that prediction which no other finite creature is able to fulfil.

It is certain, moreover, that some men have an experience which leads them to suspect the existence of a strange power; a power of intuitively perceiving what is passing in the mind of another. Indeed, that which we designate—"thought-reading," may, like some forms of sense-perception, be extraordinarily exalted by intense concentration of attention. Regarding nerve-force as a special force of physical energy, we rightly deem that there is no impossibility in such an exertion from a distance as shall bring the brain of one person into direct dynamical communication with the brain of another, without the intermediation of verbal language or of movements of expression. Only great and carefully collected evidence can establish the probability and the actuality of such communication; but no man of science has a right to say "it is impossible." When established, and it appears on the road, who will be able to doubt concerning the action of will, of mind, of spirit, on matter?

Further, we find a spontaneousness in nature by which doing and not doing, permanence and change, rest and motion, birth—life—death in usual, unusual, and conflicting manners, are wrought; and these are so far analogous to miracles that, but for experience, we should declare their occurrence impossible; and are so far capable of explanation that we can confidently say—" The raising of our present human powers; a greater knowledge, use, and application of nature's forces in their co-ordinations, affinities, and repulsions; would effectuate marvels partly similar to some of the miracles recorded in Holy Scripture. The automatism and spontaneity do not reveal the miraculous process; it is not in alphabetical, but hieroglyphical writings; we learn, however, that as religion without mystery and apart from the Supernatural would be a temple without God; so nature without marvels would be work without a masterpiece. These marvels are an assurance that manna falls day by day from Heaven for nourishment of God's people in reverence and genial nobleness. The blessed gatherers of it grow higher, and become more sacred than their contemporaries. Bearing an earthly family likeness, common to their weaker brethren, they have wisdom from their Father, which gives insight whereby they know that the earth everywhere produces miracles from "the daisy and the heather-bell up unto men."

" Men, my brothers, men the workers, ever reaping something new:
That which they have done but earnest of the things that they shall do."
TENNYSON.

THOUGHT XVIII.

DWARFED MEN.

" Oh, man, born of woman! is there a heart that thinks without pity of thee? Why live long months and years in slow wasting ignominy? Why should the bloom on thy fair face be wasted, the brightness of thine eyes be quenched, and then be stony-pale as one living in death? Has not God called thee to have faith in Him, as His child, and promised that thy foot shall light on happy land, and thy eye brighten in ever-living splendour?"
—*From Note Book.*

CHRISTIANITY being the only religion which possesses internal and external evidence, convincing European intelligence, of having come from God—of being a Supernatural Religion; Christians rationally expect and accept miracles as its proper evidence and guarantee, as set forth by our Lord in reproof of His opponents—" If I had not done among them the works that no other man did, they had not had sin " (John xv. 24).

When a human being willingly gives up the bright hopes, marvellous powers, and priceless privilege of immortality; asserts that he is conscious of nothing more than matter and material mechanism in the world; and numbering himself with the lower animals, says—"We die and are no more seen;" that human being becomes, little by little, dwarfed and blind.

Blind, not discerning the various shades and grades of

existence. Blind, one would say, not so much from physical weakness—as those colour-blind persons who discern but few of the beams that light up and glorify the earth; but blind mentally, the blindness being induced through neglect of spiritual insight. That neglect rendering him incapable of far-sightedness and discernment to perceive that, according to the true science of thought, it would be impossible for human beings to create the ideas of God and of Immortality were there not in nature, and in man, signs and tokens of Divinity and Eternity.

The man is dwarfed, moreover, with the worst kind of diminishment: for he is without—or deprives himself of—that God-consciousness, those feelings of awe, those aspirations after holiness, and those yearnings for higher, truer life, which are the grand attributes of all truly great men.

We pursue the thought with a sort of semi-seriousness, and reasoning according to the principles of natural selection, rationally conduct those who desire it to irrationality: little by little, through survival of the fittest, they had acquired, by growth of intelligence, consciousness of God and of future life; but now, not advancing in that consciousness, they lose the intelligence which they had, little by little, acquired.

The process of deterioration, which eliminates the noble, may thus be traced:—A mind, for any length of time self-limited to the brute sensual range, becomes unable to rise above brute nature: cannot find the path of ascent to that high thought by which Philosophy enters Theology. If there are any human creatures, not thus self-degraded, but really, as they assert, of mere animal birth; these must be regarded as not yet human beings in fulness; but lineal and unmixed descendants from the hypothetical brute ancestors of Adam. Otherwise, they manifest a marvellous atavism; are a most interesting and striking example how loss of consciousness, as to God and future life, causes return to original stock, notwithstanding the modern advance by natural selection and special culture. We may thus scientifically account for the existence, in these days, of men who are gradually becoming extinct, already so far dead as to declare themselves, whether by ancient heredity or of modern production, soulless, utterly incapable of immortality, without sense of divinity.

The incapacity may be otherwise thought of. No brutal or human faculty of perception can, of itself, understand its own essence and nature; much less can lower beings appreciate human nature. We know that sensitive organs do not understand what perception is, and that perceptive organs do not know what intelligence is; the higher power must judge of the lower, the lower is unable to comprehend the higher; and the low can only be put to noble use by means of the high. Some senses, however, are even stronger in peculiar low cunning beasts than are the loftier analogous in high-gifted man; and mere animal senses appear to be instinctively capable of making gordian knots of fallacies, and of weaving labyrinthine nets, just as birds build nests, or as beasts dig holes to entrap their prey, or as cunning craftiness may prove a bane to nobler natures.

There are amongst these dwarfed ones some of much higher style, even of vast intellectual attainments, who profess to laugh at Christians; but very often the laugh is not of incredulity, rather a mode of turning their consciousness of spiritual inferiority into a notion or mimicry of superiority, which they insert as consolation between their laughter and the feeling of inferiority. They know that a life of mere intellect is a life not worth living. A few, however—the very best of them—are sorrowfully conscious that they ought to learn—to live—to teach—a nobler life than that. They know that there are two kingdoms of thought: in one they are to be bold inquirers, critical—even sceptical—reasoners, this is the department of the OBJECT, or object-world; the other is the INFINITE, the unseen, the future, in which they ought to glory as believers, thanksgivers, obeyers, worshippers. These are the truly conscientious, who will be with us so soon as they appreciate what Seneca declared. "Thought breaks through the ramparts of heaven; for it is never satisfied with knowing what is merely set before the senses, but demands the scrutiny of things lying beyond the confines of this world . . . . . . Nay, we are born to this end." When conscious of their high birthright, they will begin to perceive that the real verities are conclusions from what is given by the senses to what lies beyond sense. True reasoning will lead them onward from things seen to the unseen; and faith, even when implicit and obscure, be regarded as essentially the result of reason — the necessary complement of observation: that it is, therefore, disgraceful to live any longer below the powers of investigation and spiritual insight which constitute the high distinctiveness and excellence of human nature.

By way of a little mental recreation, think of the

L

twofold process by which those who assert that there are no Heavenlies, nothing but what they strike against and touch, and that they are incapable of immortality, trace their own growth: some from vegetal, some from animal germs.

They conceive, as to vegetal germs, that the seed originated from the active conjunction of certain forces of the Earth by medium of the Sun's radiation. From and by this influx, arose a varied vegetative progression; then, after many ages, multiplying by propagation and advancing from seed to seed; ultimately a shoot appears, which is, as it were, a fœtus; a stem, as it were, a body; branches, as it were, a top or head. New seeds lie stored up in them, they are prolific, concentrate their whole energy and life on rooting in the earth, branching, and fruiting.

The other advance, that from protozoid, begins with the first vital generating plastic forces evoked from the earth, or given, by means of the sun; which then, with diversity not accounted for, pass from vegetal processes into the little granular cells of animal embryos. In some, animal life is persistently protoplasmic, it does not differentiate into various tissues; in others it does, and these ascend through sponges, hydras, corals, to the highest radiata. Some form long chains of segments, and others are non-segmented—as the snail. Some of the segmented forms change the position of their mouth, and acquire an unjointed axis which runs through all their segments; besides the little rows of ganglia they have a continuous neural axis; and thus become vertebrata. Near the top of this group are the Lemurs, above them the Monkeys, at the top Man: it is confidently asserted that *he* sprang from *them* in the direct line of ascent.

The preceding does not sufficiently or accurately represent the present scientific arrangement of the inferred progression. Take, therefore, in all seriousness, another standpoint.

Consider the present animal kingdom as a large tree, with branches and twigs to the very root, whence it goes down into depths of time and elements invisible.

Let this tree be supposed to have all but its terminal twigs invisible (extinct). In imagination, however, bring it forth to view as a sort of arboreal ghost.

The visible existing forms of life are most numerous, much specialized, and cannot pass the one to the other. There has been a gulf of special difference placed between them.

Trace them back into the tree, and they become fewer, are more and more alike, and are more generalized: especially so the nearer we come to the great branches which grow right out from the main stem.

Examples showing this—the sheep, goat, antelope, deer, ox, pig, camel, horse, rhinoceros, hippopotamus, elephant—these are modern, specialized, culminating types, with huge highly-convoluted brain, many specializations of the digestive organs, and increasing complexity of the tooth-pattern.

All this difference dies out as we descend to the depths of the Tertiary strata. Gradually the brain becomes small, and reptilian, with few convolutions; the tooth-pattern is more and more simple; and the distinction between odd-toed, even-toed (with three or four toes more or less developed), and pentadactyle types, disappears: moreover, the horse and ass abort all but the middle toe. The elephant's trunk shortens—ring by ring, the ram and antelope lose their horns, deer have no antlers, and all kinds of the great herbivora approximate to the Tapiroid type now confined to South America and Malaisia.

The above is known fact, and is becoming clearer day by day. North American Palæontology is teeming with evidence of this kind, once only known to us by European fossils.

As to the kith of man, the Primates, the lowest types exist mainly in the southern hemisphere—the home of low forms. They have smooth small brains like those of rabbits and guinea-pigs, and are so generalized that they stand in affinity to squirrels and bats, as well as to the higher apes and monkeys. These forms, the Lemurs and Flying Cats, afford no light whatever whereby we can find the supposed human ancestors. They seem, indeed, to be arrested, low forms, of one common stock of the Primates; but that is mere conjecture.

We are not yet ready for more than the most cautious tentative hypothesis. So far from being able to ascend from the monad to man, it is probable that every creature now living has lost all the members of its direct line of ancestry. A friend, W. Kitchen Parker, F.R.S., says—" We may liken the present animal creation to a high staircase: monad the first step, Homo the top one. Homo, however, does not—nor as for that do the others—appear to have gone up obliquely, but vertically; as if the staircase had been constructed perpendicularly, and all the substructure taken away afterwards;

for it is all gone." How man rose up in the grand old garden our science cannot explain. The vaunted statements and drawings of the genealogical tree are mere devices. We must use the most general and elastic language, and not allow sheep, antelopes, monkeys, and men to run foul of each other genetically. Looking down from the height of our ascent, it behoves us not to become dizzy, lest we fall and wallow in a materialistic slough. We are rather to go on rejoicing in our Heavenly destiny and the gift of immortality. We have waited a whole eternity to be born, and now, being born, a whole eternity waits to see what we will do. Shall we make it a mass of foul loss and disappointment? To the Thinker most of us present tragedy enough. Would that we remembered, "la carrière ouverte aux talens," the tools are to him who can handle them. We are not mere children of the Earth, to sink and die, we are capable of more than that—the heights of bliss and honour. Nature is our step-mother, and she is prodigal enough of gifts: by "scattering from a single Oak-tree, as provender for pigs, what would plant the whole Planet into an oak-forest," she shows, by that prodigality, what superabundance must be the possession of men who are gifted above all other earthly existences. It is time that we rouse ourselves—be true to our great estate, and remember—the real quality of our insight, of our strength: the mental strength to comprehend and use the nature of a thing, specially of a human being, depends on the faith, lovingness, truth, patience, with which we diligently use our whole man. Intellect comes from the whole man, and is the lamp of God to enlighten the whole man.

THOUGHT XIX.

MECHANICAL VIEW OF THE WORLD.

" By sagacious windings and gradual insinuations you may so turn weak understandings that they will turn truth into error; turn fairest sunshine into blackest night, and purest goodness into foulest wickedness."

From Note Book.

IF we regard the world as a mechanism, it possesses endless levers, infinite wheels, marvellous cranks, and innumerable springs. It contains, within itself, continuative and compensative powers. Now it is evident, that if we adhere to mechanical science in our interpretation, it is impossible for any mechanism to call itself into being: that is, begin to act before it has any existence.

The world may be likened to a building, and we may think of the atoms and molecules self-positing themselves; may think of stone fitting to stone, and buttresses supporting the whole, by means of molecular affinities and repulsions. It is clear, however, that unless we impart something more than mechanical action to the materials—endue them with the skill and foresight of an architect—the building will be without design and adjustment, will not form one grand unity, but be a gathering or a scattering in uttermost medley of confusion.

Thought of as a Tree, or a Living Organism, it seems impossible that by self-origination, without seed, planting, or designing, the world should be endowed with productive, reproductive, and all other energies; roots, stems, branches, twigs, leaves, blossoms, fruit, being of spontaneous growth.

Whether as a Mechanism, or Building, or an Organism, the world could not originate itself. The only escape from the conclusion that a Designer, a Builder, a Creator, gave the world its being; is found in the possibility that nature, or the world, may be eternal. There is a difficulty, seeing that the universe is unique, in ascertaining at once and unmistakably whether it is so or not. The world being one; cannot be compared with another; and some men think that the ascription of eternity can neither be annulled nor affirmed. Most men are not of that opinion: it is generally thought to be a matter not beyond our knowledge; and that the materials for adequate knowledge are furnished by the world itself; we, therefore, endeavour to obtain a reasonable and scientific opinion for ourselves; give the hypothesis, as to eternity, a fair statement; and contrast it, in every part, with whatever facts seem to prove that there was a creation.

I. Materialistic Hypothesis.

The universe has not existed always in its present form: but in continual origination, progression, and decay; new worlds succeeding old worlds; restoration being effected by fresh use of worn-out materials. The primal or ultimate matter, from which the various suns and planets were formed, being universally—not necessarily equally—diffused, is to be accounted structureless, without parts or properties; or right may be claimed to assume, if needful, that the atoms, as we know them with all their attributes, are eternal; moving eternally in a perfect fluid — that is, a fluid without friction.

Refutation :—Given the atoms without their properties, no merely mechanical theory, apart from creative power, accounts for motion in a perfect fluid; it could not be in one part more than in another; nor could it at any time, or in any part, mechanically begin, for there is no reason why it should begin or exist, at any one time or part, more than in another. Given the atoms with their properties, motions may be set up, atoms rush together and form molecules; but the motion, caused by attraction of gravity, proceeds in a straight line—making units to strike one against another, then to set off in another direction, until again striking, they take a third direction, and so on. It is not, however, possible to construct the manifold circular, spiral, and other exceedingly complex world-motions, out of any, even infinite, number of small or large straight lines. It seems, moreover, impossible for these movements, and counter movements, attractions and repulsions, to be in operation without exciting that friction which, retarding motion, would certainly produce equilibrium—bring everything to a standstill. If no perfect fluid exists, or if friction is caused in it, motion from eternity to eternity is utterly impossible by mere mechanical action. The universe, then, cannot possibly have been eternal in the past; nor will it be eternal in the future—if it rested or has to rest on pure mechanical action.

The Refutation may be stated more briefly, thus—

If we admit, and we must on materialistic principles, that physical laws remain for ever unchanged (no change being possible except by creative power) we know, as well as we can know anything, that the present order of things has not been evolved through infinite past ages by the agency of laws now at work, but must have had a distinct beginning—a beginning produced by other than the now visibly acting causes; therefore, the ice of our winters, and the construction of our globe, had their origin in a different state of things to that now existing; "a state of things incapable of being derived by present laws (of tangible matter and its energy) from any conceivable present arrangement."

II. Materialistic Hypothesis.

The grand progression from the inorganic to the organic is by mechanical force. The architecture of a grain of wheat resembles the molecular formation of a crystal, and is by the same laws; the molecules of the corn being self-posited by the forces with which they act on one another. "The animal body is just as much the product of molecular force as the stalk and ear of corn, or as the crystal of salt or sugar." It follows that, not by means of a supernatural agent, but by energy derived from the sun, animals and plants obtain all their forces; the building up of the vegetable being effected by the sun through the reduction of chemical compounds, and the phenomena of animal life being more or less complicate reversals of those processes of reduction.

Refutation:—Light and heat are produced by the impact of dead matter, but not without the energy of that impact; from the light and heat, thus produced, are said to be derived the energies called vital, but not without the energy arising from impact with some other inner motion. In vain do light and heat knock at the door, as is proved by experiment, unless there be a conjunction, an afflux and influx from above or within, below or without, of the mysterious energy that produces a living force. The proof is easy. Take the eye as an illustration; in vain light pierces through the crystalline humour and lenses, and is carried along the fibres into minutest lamina of the retina; in vain images present themselves in all variations of light and shade; without energy to meet all these, there will be no ocular sight; without some organic principles, some vital, discriminating, rational influx or afflux, there will be no rational sight. There is, therefore, something more in life, in intellect, than solar energy can account for. Taking the very lowest view—"Molecular forces determine the form which the solar energy will assume." These molecular forces separating carbon and oxygen, do, by connection with the organic principle, whatever that may be, build up a cabbage or an oak. In like manner, by reunion of the carbon and of the oxygen, the molecular machinery, combining with the infinitely modifying organic principle or energy, weaves the texture of a frog, or elaborates the form of a man. The conclusion is, we do not derive all our energies from a sun-god, we possess molecular potentialities, and manifold organic principles, which the solar energy is incompetent to explain.

Professor Tyndall stated (Belfast Address, p. 29), that he discerned in matter "the promise and the potency of every form and quality of life." This, so far as true, may mean that which is taught in Scripture (Gen. i. 11, 20, 24). Probably, the Professor would have us understand that the potency is from the Almighty; specially as he states (p. 30), "It is by the operation of an insoluble mystery that life is evolved, species differentiated, and mind unfolded;" but many infer from his words that he considers life and intelligence to be properties of special forms of matter; we, however, cannot understand how he could see the promise and potency of that about which he knows nothing—see the germs of the operation and evolution of that which is an "insoluble mystery." In fact most of these professional and presidential addresses, the hard words crystallization, fermentation, germination, are only a circumlocutory elegant form of expression for that ugly word "ignoramus." It is time for commonsense people to understand that when very clever men say, "Suns resolve themselves into floræ and faunæ, that is into vegetables and animals," they only mean that the natural forces used by the Almighty are, so far as physically known, derived from terrestrial and solar sources; and that it is impossible to give an exhaustive account of any one of the changes characteristic of any living thing in nature.

Taking the assertion, that without any exercise of Divine Mind, or direction of controlling Intelligence, "the grand progression from the inorganic to the organic is by mechanical force," we will carry it into the region of practice.

We leave everything to its own so called natural organization, continuative, and progressive powers. Will crab-stocks grow into apple-trees; and the common sloe turn, of itself, into all the rich varieties of plums ? Will the wild rose, by self-planting and automatic progress, attain the delicious fragrance, graceful form, delicate colours, and unrivalled beauty possessed by the queen of flowers? Can our breeders of stock leave the choice of "short-horns," and "south-downs," to "natural selection?" Will noblemen allow their stud of hunters, or the members of the Jockey Club leave their blood-horses, to progress by natural equine development? Certainly not. So far from nature turning the roadster into a racer, and the hack into a hunter, she will lead them back towards the original stock. Nature does not help the cattle-breeder and feeder by always putting flesh of best quality in the right place; and giving to bone firmest yet lightest form conjoined with greatest strength. The gardener, by care and skill, planting, grafting, budding, fertilization, use of new seeds, fresh stocks, various adaptations, forcings and crossings, must wisely and carefully cultivate: or plants, far from advancing, will return to primitive stage; and obscure colour, faint scent, woolly taste, will rebuke the folly that trusted to natural selection and inherent power to advance in strength and clothe with beauty. A thoughtful mind discerns that in nature which seems intended to call out human effort; discerns that inner potentiality which greeted by human intelligence—not otherwise—waxes good, great, and blesses the skilfully diligent with rich increase. Such advance can hardly be called mechanical, the process is rather an intellectual achievement by use of material means, and seems contrived by Intelligence to prove that origin, growth, and advance, are not by an unaided automatic process.

III. **Materialistic Hypothesis.**

The substances in organic bodies are primarily inorganic, as all forces are mechanical; therefore, the forces of organic matter are not different in kind from those of inorganic matter. "It is the compounding in the organic world of forces belonging equally to the inorganic that constitutes the mystery and the miracle of vitality."

Refutation :—Organic bodies are not only inorganic matter and its forces, but all these—plus the organic construction and energy : therefore, an organism is possessed of more than the forces of inorganic matter ; and the marvellous nature and power of this "more" may be seen by comparing a living man with a dead body. An intelligent organism is more wonderful than one merely vital : it is an organism plus emotion, intelligence, awe ; with all those manifold faculties, responsibilities, fears and hopes, sorrows and joys, thereto belonging.

The conclusion is irresistible : a merely mechanical theory does not adequately explain either the eternity of the world, or its origin within time ; it does not reveal the mystery of the great progression of life from the inorganic to the organic ; it does not afford a sufficiently accurate or comprehensive view of vitality, and is utterly incompetent to explain the deeper mystery of mind. Those materialists who adopt Kant's words—"Give me matter and I will explain the formation of a world ;" must add his other words—generally omitted—"but give me matter only and I cannot explain the formation of a caterpillar." Our present science proves that the universe, as now looked upon, is not eternal ;

science is unable to explain either the eternity, or creation of matter; can throw no real light on the origination of motion, of life, of intelligence; for that motion should begin, of itself, in absolute equilibrium; that life should be a son of death; that intelligence should be the intelligent product of unintelligent fortuity—are things utterly incredible. We must dismiss the mechanical theory, as an explanation of the universe apart from Deity and Creation, as intellectually absurd and physically impossible.

We give matter to the Materialist, but he can do nothing with it, owing to inertia. What is inertia? incapacity to originate force, or motion. We will go further—give matter, endowed with all its present properties, but the gift is profitless: for as everything is tending to equilibrium, or eternal stand-still—coldness—deadness it is evident—that which is unable to continue motion, heat, life, through an eternal future, cannot have possessed them eternally in the past, or have voluntarily assumed them.

Let him who would construct a Godless world arouse from that delusion of sin and folly. Of all feelings, states, principles, in the mind of man, Faith is the clearest, purest, strongest, best; a lasting Faith is perennial joy to the whole man, blessing body, soul, and spirit. Let him have faith in that Divine Mind, that Holy God, who is the Absolute, the Eternal, Self-existing Being, Who by voluntary, creative, concrete conception, makes Eternity and Infinitude, the worlds and marvels therein contained, the child of His intellect—the fruit of His act. This sublime recognition of Deity, as the sender forth of the stupendous mechanism of the starry systems, infinite in their extent and trackless in the depths of space; of Deity, as forming within every atom of matter—every particle of vital substance—every germ of intelligence—its own entity and potentiality, making every one a little world; is the true human conception of Creator and Creation. Then, in the Universal, will open depths, which, leading within, conduct our reverential wondering thoughts to the inner secret recesses— springs of things—where are realms of spirit opening inward, ever more and more, until we pause to adore that Glorious One, Who has opened within the universal height and depth, length and breadth, other universes; so that realms and realms do hide and contain themselves in less than microscopic points.

Who can measure the meaning of these intensive and extensive influences? Our science, our literature, will pass away; Europe, the Earth, the Universe, will pass away; fade as a cloud speck from out the azure sky. Are we lost for ever? Nay. We give to matter all those forces called physical, all those operations called chemical, all those principles called vital, all those energies called mental. Then we liken the spread-out matter to the solid foot-board; the mountains, raised up, to the organ-stops; the trees of a thousand forests, to pipes; the wide ocean-swellings to the wind, to great bellows; all living things, to the key-board. Complicate mechanical arrangements are physical properties, rendered living and mental by life and intelligence. Thus, the Earth, aye the Universe, is a splendid musical instrument—the Almighty's grand organ. The correspondence of part to part was designed; the music, however wild some of the melodies, was composed—a better than Beethoven's spirit indwelling. What then is man? He endures but an hour, some say; but in the being, existence, and doing of a faithful man is something that pertains not to the region of death-element; something that even now conquers time—possessing, in thought, the eternal lying behind, the eternal stretching out before; something that reverently approaches, and possesses God, by a Divinity of life—of thought—of emotion—so that he rejoices in the glorious anthems and oratorios of Creation and Redemption; and knows that they will be rendered complete by the swelling harmony of Heaven.

THOUGHT XX.

KNOWLEDGE COMES BUT WISDOM LINGERS.

"No wonder that those who would have us believe that the highest aspirations of the soul are but so many manifestations of units of force, desire to chain the mind so close to the material, that it shall no longer be able to exercise one of its remarkable endowments—that of leading towards regions where the senses cannot penetrate."—DR. BEALE.

WISDOM sees that there is some grand, far-off event unto which all things are tending; and wisdom matures men for this wonderful ripening of time. Knowledge, when apart from wisdom, seems to find but has still to seek; makes acquaintance with parts, yet does not give them life and organization; and seeking to undo one old riddle—"how things are done"—propounds a hundred new. Natural knowledge is the handmaid that prepares for wisdom, and though dwelling on life's lower phase, does not knit men, already half akin, to the beast, but finds that seed of higher life which wisdom cultures into flower and fruit. Wisdom, looking eye to eye with knowledge, discerns the links which unite every form of being, every movement of life, every action of intelligence, every day of time, into that grand wave of existence—of vitality—of mind—of duration—proceeding through Infinitude as the life-throb of Him who is the Absolute, All In All. By this eyesight and insight, wisdom enables the willing and capable to acquire the energy befitting those who are called to the great offices of ministration by which they prepare their weaker brethren for the grand destiny which awaits our race.

The errors of knowledge, apart from wisdom, in forgetting that things

> "Are not what they seem,
> And other than the forms we touch,"—

may be observed in some professedly accurate physical statements.

"When hydrogen and oxygen are mixed in a certain proportion, and an electric spark is passed through them, they disappear, and a quantity of water, equal to the sum of their weights, appears in their place .... Is the case in any way changed when carbonic acid, water, and ammonia disappear, and in their place, under the influence of the pre-existing protoplasm, an equivalent weight of the matter of life makes its appearance? ... If the properties of water may be properly said to result from the nature and disposition of its compound molecules, I can find no intelligible ground for refusing to say that the properties of protoplasm result from the nature and disposition of its molecules."

This professes to be a thorough and an accurate statement, as to water and protoplasm, which we are bound to accept—" if scientific language is to possess a definite and constant signification." We maintain the very opposite: it is inaccurate and unscientific. For example: —The properties of water do not result merely from the nature and disposition of hydrogen and oxygen; but also from an alteration in their nature and disposition effected by the passing through them of an electric spark.

The same error is in the statement as to protoplasm. Carbonic acid, water, and ammonia, do not produce life by the nature and disposition of their molecules; nor do they ever produce an equivalent weight of the matter of life—the matter of life is a very much more complicate substance. Combine these elements in any way that science directs, they remain dead, not the least life is in them. So far from possessing life—carbonic acid, water, and ammonia cannot, by any process that we are acquainted with, be made into protoplasm; and if made, even then, they would be as far from life as the Earth is from the Sun; for protoplasm is never made to live without the action of pre-existent life. Every living organism possesses mechanical relations, those called chemical, and the vital: without the vital, no organism can exist.

That within the essential unity of all life are many germs of wholly different natures, seems established by the fact that hybrids, offspring from the union of different species, are mostly sterile. It is also known that as the germs become organisms, the use of an organ may account for its modification, not for its origin: for it cannot be used until it is formed. It is further known, that many animals possess organs and peculiarities which are rather a hindrance than an advantage in the struggle for existence. These facts prove that Natural Selection, though exercising great influence, does not account for all the varieties in life. This knowledge has not yet brought wisdom: for some among us believe that, though nature is unable of herself to make large leaps, she can do the impossible by means of little jumps.

For our own part, we will endeavour to arrange well-considered facts in such manner that by aid of wisdom we may ascertain the true life-plan.

Variation is due to inner and outward force, to sexual selection, use, misuse, and disuse of parts; but these account only for some, not for all modifications. Life did not exist when our earth was in a gaseous state. Indeed the gaseous state, itself, is called in question: for how could gases be made solid, and yet contain considerable heat? Nor could life, as now known, exist on the earth when the metals were fused; nor could a cooling planet—simply because it was cooling—make a cell or tiny house for life's first habitation. It is not in the power of time to enable nothing to turn into something; nor is infinitude wide enough, apart from life somewhere, to find a place in which dead matter may, of itself, begin to live, turn round, and clothe itself with intelligence. All this wisdom accepts as knowledge.

We have no evidence, direct or indirect, that spontaneous generation ever occurred. Even if protoplasm, a compound of C H N O and sulphur, could be produced by synthesis; it would not be alive, nor possess the powers of living protoplasm. It is against all experience and analogy of nature, that spontaneous generation ever did occur within the present range and state of things; and the law of science is that variability, being a lessening, is a finite quantity; and we are fairly sure that the very small finite quantity, of the initial life of lowest forms did not contain the potentiality of highest life in noblest forms. This may be shown:—in one generation, even, there may be a sudden and total return to the original stock; consequently, sufficient time for evolution of many would also afford that space in which involution would cause all to return; therefore, the existing marvellous varieties could not have sprung from any low primary germ—supposing that such had ever been spontaneously evolved—they must have had their own original essential principles limiting the range, capabilities and duration of existence. It is certain that advance has not been universal: the trilobite, amongst the most ancient of fossil forms, had eyes fully developed and perfect. The nautilus of to-day is no advance on that of the world's early ages. The brain of man, in earliest skulls, is larger than he needed for mere living. The cubic capacity of ape brain is thirty-four inches; of lowest human brain, sixty-eight; the skeleton throughout is made and adjusted for erect position; and the fore-limbs, wholly raised above the ground, are adapted to other and higher use than that of locomotion. That some marvellous design, some all-embracing teleology, governs all this, may be seen by a striking example. There is a marvellous arrangement for the fertilization of orchids: in one species of these flowers the sipping moths "are purposely delayed in obtaining nectar," and Dr. Darwin says—"If this is accidental, it is a fortunate accident for the plant. If this be not accidental, and I cannot believe it to be accidental, what a singular case of adaptation!" Evidently there are unseen and abiding realities underlying all passing appearance: God has no meaningless words.

The Theory of Evolution, so far as it passes into actual verified science, is very beautiful. It proves that the Creator's plan was more wonderful than we thought, and it enlarges our knowledge of the marvellous processes. It is certain—if diffused mist was an aggregate of matter, of life, of intelligence, of all that goes to making of the universe; then all past evolution, and all future evolution, represent that creation, and form that true equation, which gives concrete form to the power, will, and wisdom of the Almighty.

View this more simply, and in detail—There must be a cause for everything, a First Cause. Our personality, will and conscience, are not of our own making: they spring from a prior personality, will, and conscience. If chemical units combine into units infinitely more complex, the complex unity contains more than the mere mechanical bringing together of the component parts. If physiological units, formed by these chemical units, possess distinctive power and proceed to the composition of separate organisms; that does not endow material atoms with inherent wisdom, life, and force—as were they little gods; we regard the marvel as a phenomenon or embodiment of the Unknown energy that fills the universe. Rock crystal on one side, and vegetable organism on the other; animal sensation here, and human intelligence there; life weaving all things that live, intelligence guiding all that think; movements apart from life and intelligence, condensation of gas or vapour into fluid or solid—assuming scores of shapes, and moving to and fro; are all by appointment: some stand out apart, as far-off stars gleaming in the sky; and every, even the smallest, has reasonable place.

The Materialist does not discern this; and, though the qualities of matter and mind are the antipodes of one another, he speaks of them " as one substance with two sets of properties, two sides, the physical and the mental, a double-faced unity." " If any one had said to Newton," we use the words of Augustus De Morgan ("Budget of Paradoxes," p. 92), "'I hold that every particle of matter is a responsible being of vast intellect, ordered by the Creator to move as it would do if every other particle attracted it, and gifted with power to make its way in true accordance with that law, as easily as a lady picks her way across the street : what have you to say against it ?' Newton must have replied, 'Sir! if you really undertake to maintain this as *demonstrable*, your soul had better borrow a little power from the particles of which your body is made : if you merely ask me to refute it, I tell you I neither can nor need do it; for whether attraction comes in this way or in any other, *it comes*, and that is all I have to do with it.'"

The Materialist knows very well that we cannot speak of thought and emotion, pleasure and pain, as if inertia, form, outline, and division of parts belonged to them ; knows that there cannot co-inhere in the same substance extension and absence of extension, inertia and the absence of inertia, colour—form—and the absence of colour and form ; yet we are asked to believe that a thing can be and not be at the same time, and in the same sense; that the horse and the rider are identical. See the crawling caterpillar, now it is a chrysalis, in a little while it is a beautiful butterfly ; it is the same being, yet not the same ; and we are the same beings despite our many bodily changes. The butterfly, chrysalis, caterpillar, are productions of partly visible, partly invisible process; our own change is mostly invisible—but as we are conscious that all things are woven by something not themselves, linking them to the transcendental, we are possessed with an assurance that our weaving and linking are still more wonderful—by One Most Wonderful.

Knowledge, when apart from wisdom, goes astray as to sensation and mental activity; asserting that they are wholly wrought by physical changes; though, in reality, we know nothing whatever of the mysterious operation which translates material vibrations into sensation, intelligence and emotion; and are ignorant of the way in which Light produces Chemical change, and Chemical change excites Nerve-force. All that we know is a succession of sequences; nevertheless, from this, of which nothing is known, Materialists argue that as the sensation of light follows the formation of a luminous image on the retinæ, and as the sensation of hearing is a consequence of pulsation on the auditory nerves, there is a correlation between sensation—the primary state of mental activity, and all following stages of mental activity. Hence, the translations of physical vibrations by means of physiological instrumentality, concerning which nothing is known beyond the fact of antecedent and consequent, are to be taken as explanation of something altogether different; for it is not the ear that hears, nor the eye that sees, but the intellect which uses them as instruments. Intellect is not the mechanism which it uses, sensation is not the antecedent pulsation, any more than man is the machine by which he works, or time is the watch with which we measure it.

The forces of the outer and inner worlds, of physical

and mental states, possess some correlation, but do not assimilate either to other. We are in the midst of perpetual changes, alike in the external and inner worlds, of which we can discover neither the beginning nor the end. After all that has been said, the ultimate mystery remains just as it was: explanation only shows that it is inexplicable. Speaking is not thought, nor is thought a modification of matter. Mental analysis may bring us down to sensation, as something near to the original materials out of which thought is woven, but that does not forward us; seeing that we cannot in the least comprehend sensation, nor even conceive how sensation is possible. Two things may conjoin as to succession, yet one is not as the other: they may be far apart as life from death, as action from repose, as day from night. There may be appearances, we see not; no appearances, and we see. The blind as to natural sight, see in their dreams; and some, whose organs of sense are torpid or dead, are at times quick-sighted, and perceive and know without the usual percipient organs. Physicists cannot give any explanation of these marvels: for though some Materialists pretend that the phenomena observed in a living thing, or in a bit of living matter, can be explained by known laws, they do not even attempt to account for the changes characteristic of any one living thing. They cannot throw any light whatever upon the cause of the vibration of a single cilium, cannot imitate the phenomena which occur in the simplest form of living matter.

This is truly marvellous, but we may obtain higher thoughts. Consider Life: not as a watch, nor as any mere mechanism, dissipating the low and common form of energy contained in a coiled spring: think that every, even the smallest, part of the living organism is using up its own little store of energy, and is constantly replenished from external sources drawn upon by the arrangements and harmonious working of the whole organism: make, if you can, at least in your imagination, a duck like that of Vaucanson—to walk, to fly, to partake of food. Then suppose that every part, even those excessively small, is microscopically constructed and perfect as the whole. You are still very far from the living reality; its instinct, its portion of intelligence, its hidden vitality, are utterly unattainable. Then, if you think further, you will find that on a graduated scale there can be as many divisions between unity and nothing, as between unity and infinity. Call your own degree of consciousness unity: there may be as many existing different degrees below your own, as there are above it, rising to the most exalted mind. Those who assert that there are no miracles do but babble. Matter is full of miracles, life is full of miracles, mind is full of miracles, and within the minutest particles is an inner world, beautiful and wonderful as all the great surrounding spheres.

The inorganic substance, so soon as life enters, even of lowest form, is built up into the plant. The organic substance, so soon as intelligence enters, even in its lowest form, is woven into the animal texture. The blending of matter, of life, of intelligence, are a wonderful trinity; and the three are one in man. His frame contains the material substance, the life-energy, the mental principle, a trinity of being. Let him who has wisdom carry this trinity to its types in the Eternal Essence. Think that there are three moments of development : the objective presentment, or embodiment ; the differentiation into manifold complex forms ; the carrying these into co-ordination, or correspondence, with the perfection of the Organizer. Presentment, or embodiment, is the bringing into existence the elements of the universe. Differentiation affords the possibility, where freedom exists, of aberration or divergence. The co-ordination is not only a Redemption, but an Elevation, or sanctifying of things which have been differentiated into higher and higher being continually. These stages are evidence of design, and design has beginning and a contemplated end. Omnipotence and Omniscience seem so to have planned the creation, continuance and exaltation of beings and existences, that from rudest elements, lowest life, least intelligence, there shall—by intervening steps of action and progress—be a marvellous elevation in such manner that every individual, while tasting precious life, will be enabled to render it more precious by a conscious voluntary co-operation with the power and grace of the Eternal, so as to pass into something better and higher. St. Paul exclaims in wonderment—"O the depth of the riches both of the wisdom and knowledge of God! how unsearchable are His judgments, and His ways past finding out" (Rom. xi. 33).

Now change the matter and manner of thought. Pass from thousands of molecular and nervous fibres, thousands of blood vessels, thousands of co-operations in the lungs—in the heart—in the brain—in the spinal cord ; from action to sensation, from sensation to mental process, from mental process to spiritual capacity ; to the inner man, which makes man to be himself. You perceive, by careful observation, that the impressions made by outward material things are not the only bases of sensation, perception, remembrance; nor do motions and modifications of matter necessarily cause thought; nor is the nature of mind, or of life—though resting on and joined with matter—essentially material. There are merely a correspondence and conjunction.

Continuing the thought, we find that the properties and operations of matter being known by external apprehension; the faculties and acts of the mind being known by internal apprehension; we are conscious of the outer and the inner. How the physical processes are connected with consciousness we cannot say; but, as no effect is without cause, we may be sure that the present constitution of human nature—particularly as to highest operations of intellect and emotion, combining recollections of the past and expectations of the future—rests on something permanent; on something not atomic, but having unity; on something possessing mystical organic union, continuous as the thread of a necklace; something steady in our fleeting life, standing in the horizon of existence as the rainbow, though the drops of rain ever and rapidly change their position.

By means of this permanency, continued consciousness of identity, we may establish a connection with other states and modes of being. The following facts are offered as simply suggestive to any one capable of continuing the investigation. In the human frame we possess net-work within net-work. Every web of tissues taken separately, represents the human form: place by itself the bony structure, then the muscular portion; apart and by themselves, in order, the veins and arteries, with the white form of nerves held up. More ethereal than this bony mechanism, than the ghost of nervous structure, is the invisible inner man of all. This inner man and outer man, the spirit and body, acting in diversity and in unity, by complicity of organs and dual distribution, from side to side, to and from the nervous centres, render probable the existence of a remarkable subtle fluid essence, invisibly present, as the means whereby the functions of soul and body, of spirit and matter, are performed. It is not to be defined as essentially material, but regarded as the medium for acts of consciousness.

We possess evidence as to the existence of something somewhat analogous, of an all-pervading substance, æther; the medium of light, heat, electricity, perhaps of gravitation and magnetism; one of the most subtle and universal elements of the universe. Without it, we should not see—nor be warmed—the sun's light and heat would be in vain. This æther is not the air which we breathe, but it pervades every part of our bodies, is higher and purer than the atmosphere. It is, to say the least, probable that another æther, so we may call it, exists as a medium uniting our consciousness, or mental nature, to the physical constitution; and by means of it the instinct of animals may act. Some able men further assert that by means of a yet purer aura the Most Holy God exerts, for ever and ever, His influence over spiritual existences.

The exercise of thought in this manner enables our mind to ascend from realm to realm of higher spirituality; until the universe becomes an infinite, all-sided spiral, ascending from glory to glory, from heaven to heaven; until, like St. Paul, we behold we that which are not able to utter. Even if it be true that only the highest style of men are likely to attain such knowledge; we may any of us possess that wisdom which, better than knowledge, prepares us for the wonderful state in which these high things will be subjects of daily experience. This may be viewed from another stand-point.

If, as some assert, our nerves of sensation are positive and the nerves of motion negative, we possess an inner electric telegraph, with some subtle fluid-affluent or influent, with life and enlightenment for the whole man. Suppose that gravity is the pressure of æther, gravity acting by transmission from within and without, is the intervening and welding medium of all worlds and of all things; anyhow, we obtain foundation for thought; and may at some distant time know what it is that affects the correlation of physical force and mental emotion, of Divine Will and physical operation. Meanwhile, we are content to know that the natural and Supernatural, man and God, matter and Spirit, will some day be brought into beautiful, wonderful, miraculous accord.

THOUGHT XXI.

HUMAN-WISE.

"Whatever it may be for which man feels his combination of love, trust and awe, carried to the highest limits of which his nature is capable; this, and nothing else, is the object of his highest worship."—EDWIN A. ABBOTT, D.D.

SOME of the irreligious, happily, are wearied with the miseries of their dismal science. They break in upon physical studies by some nobler inquiries, and find the interruption no hindrance. They act upon Lord Bacon's direction—"Let not a man force a habit upon himself with a perpetual continuance: but with some intermission. For both the pause reinforceth the new onset; and if a man that is not perfect be ever in practice, he shall as well practise his errors as his abilities." These honest inquirers are told by those less in earnest—"To speak of God as were He a Person is anthropomorphic; and to believe in miracles renders nature imperfect, as if it needed adjustment."

Such language produces a deterrent effect even upon intelligent persons. We, therefore, state the true facts of the case: showing that our opponents, refusing high and true anthropomorphism, fall into the low and wrong.

The low and wrong sort of anthropomorphism likens nature to a building, or to a tree, or to a machine; as if nature's work, God's work, was not higher, better, more than any of these. To be rid of a Divine beginning, it asserts—" There never was a beginning, only transformations of motion," as if this were not babble mainly. To be rid of Divine Providence and Design—the miseries of men and groanings of creation, noxious animals and all evil things are paraded; and paraded with the intent that sacredness be taken from the pathos of our life, and awe from our silent death. Now this is the very worst kind of anthropomorphism, that kind indeed which is opposed even to good taste, and natural feeling: for we cannot see the summer gloaming steal over the moorland, we cannot receive light from the pleasant skies, and listen to nature's endless tunes; without in some degree getting pious profit, so that we face them solemnly.

The low sort of anthropomorphism, takes the outer form of man, the material and sensual organism, and counts it the whole man. Forgets or denies the inner principle—from which the outer grew; is unmindful of the mystic person—which extracted the material person from outer substances, and likens God — not to a Ruler, but to the forces of matter; to matter itself—not to a Person, our highest possible conception of being and existence; and to space in which matter moves—irrationally diffusing Divinity, not glorifying Him as the Eternal, the Infinite, the Omniscient, the Almighty. This is low indeed.

The low anthropomorphism takes that clothing which life assumes in progressing from the inorganic to the organic, from plant to beast of the field, and from beast of the field to man, as were that clothing and the putting of it on—life itself. The professors of this system do not discern the difference between the plastic principle, and plastic materials; between the invisible building power, and the house it builds: consequently they confound the thousands of muscular fibres, thousands of nervous fibres, thousands of blood-vessels, thousands of operations in lungs, heart, brain, spinal cord; with the essentiality of a human being. No wonder that the God of such a system is no God, is nothing apart from the world; as man, so they represent, is nothing apart from the body.

This seems a little too bad; and, to amend it, they put forth an amusing dogma. There is somewhere in the world a maximum finite brain, a highest finite intelligence in the universe—or else several, all equal. This is the clearest and sublimest of all their verities: there is somewhere at this present moment in our planet, or in some other habitable orb, the very highest intelligence and will in the universe; but it is well-nigh impossible for us to know who he is, and he most assuredly cannot know that the crown is on his head. So they construct a non-natural man, dropping out all they account weakness, and inserting all that they deem strong. This magnified man they worship. Shall we Christians be ashamed of the true God-man, Christ, who was, is, and ever will be first? Is not Christ better than their greatest biologist, and most prodigious physicist?

True anthropomorphism does not make a graven image of matter, erect it in space, move it with force, and say to men—" Behold thy god! see how he moves within his habitation." Those who hold true doctrine, know that Materialism, whether it appear in the old

Egyptian form, so that men worship a beetle; or in sensuous modern glorifying of "La Madre Natura;" is a degrading idolatry. True anthropomorphism is opposed to this, is a good thing. It erects in the heart an image of the Divine Person—not of the ancients' best Parian, nor of ivory, nor of gold, nor of the Materialist's coarser grit; but a spiritual image of truth, justice, wisdom, love, might. This image of the Wonderful, set up in the heart, renders the whole body a temple—the spirit an inner shrine—and the silent worship is very gladsome, yet solemn in its reverence. God is enthroned in Eternity, the I Am that I Am; established in Omnipotence, as the All in All of worlds, the conscious Ruler of whatsoever therein is.

Christ was the highest embodiment of this Holy Worship. He wonderfully taught us of it; and now, Himself, receives it from us. He, by the power of a Divine-human nature, and a human-nature Divine—or, so to speak, the humanity in God allying itself with our humanity in Christ—evoked a Faith which inspires words, creates deeds, gives endurance, that render men sublime. Confessors—maligned by emperors and princes; martyrs—suffering in the flames, torn of wild beasts, tormented by a multitude; were dauntless when alone against the world, and prevailed against every foe. Generations and generations have gone to rest, comforted by the hope of heavenly bliss; having in every spiritual pleasure a foretaste of glory. Heroic lives, of valiant daring and wonderful performance for the Almighty, knew that they should not be deprived of any glorious expectation; but find more and better than all they looked for. The weary and sad, the widow and the orphan, the weak and those for whom no man cared, knew that by the help of Jesus, they should find their way to a blessed land. This is true anthropomorphism. It is the moral, the spiritual, the heavenly impulse which Christ gave. It is miraculous in its source, and in its effects. By it we are conscious of a spiritual transportation to a Heavenly Sphere. As we advance, new regions of thought are entered; old truths take more glorious wrappings, and higher life ever and evermore grows in gladness; we are enriched with all the treasures of God.

We might leave our thought as sufficiently expressed; but the weakness is so common in the materialistic class, of regarding personality and infinity as words expressing ideas which are mutually incompatible, that we must state plainly: Personality and Infinity are compatible ideas. God as manifesting Himself in man, in a rich and powerful nature, in mighty world-events, cannot be regarded as separable from Intelligence. Intelligence contains the power of self-consciousness, of self-determination, of self-possession, this is Personality; and by it the great "I AM" regards Himself as one and the same for ever and ever.

Personality, as the very highest and most perfect form of real being, is that alone in which we can conceive highest and absolute Unity. The essential elements of it are existence, consciousness of this existence, and control over it. The question is not whether the creature is a measure of the Creator, but the fact is that we must think of God by analogy and experience of our own mind—immeasurably inferior, not essentially different. From what is best in ourselves we must reason on infinitely. The laws of the universe are an expression of the Divine working, and by analogical working of our own mind we attain the highest possible definition of the Supreme—a Person, Unknowable in His essence, known in and by His manifestations. Dwelling in man, but transcending every thought; within nature, but not by nature contained. We go forth into the still night, and regard some fixed and distant star; we reckon the millions and millions and millions of miles, and as we reckon the distance recedes further and further; it is unapproachable, it is immeasurable; yet this star affords us light and friendly presence so that we are glad in its shine. In like manner our Holy God is present in innumerable blessings, near as if we embraced Him in every lovable object; we live in Him, move in Him, are encircled by His arms, and breathed in by His Spirit; yet He remains ever that Star, that Sun, immeasurably beyond us, unto whom for ever and ever we nearer and nearer approach.

THOUGHT XXII.

LAW WITHIN THE LAW.

"A key is out of relation, either to the inside or outside taken separately out of the enclosure which it opens; but it is in relation to both taken together as being the instrument of admission from the one to the other. Take any tool or implement of art, handicraft, or husbandry, and look at it by itself; what an eccentric and unmeaning thing it is, wholly out of order and place, but it is in exact order and place as the medium between the workman and the material—and a miracle is in perfect order and place as the medium between two worlds."—J. B. MOZLEY, D.D.

WE will endeavour, in a true spirit of anthropomorphism, to arrive at a conception of Divine Personal Government.

Government and state are of two kinds: one corresponding to space, one corresponding to time. The state corresponding to space is Being. That which corresponds to time is Existence. The Infinite represents the Divine in Being. The Eternal represents the Divine in Existence. Both terms are to be understood in a supreme sense: apart from space and apart from time.

Nature is the recipient of space—that is Being; and the recipient of time—that is Existence: everything that is in nature being and existing by an immaterial principle—law within the law. Men are beings—that is, constituted for space; and are existences—that is, constituted as to time. The hypothesis is fundamental:

gradation is everywhere, and in all similarity is diversity; in the little and in the great, in the microcosm and macrocosm, in Heaven and in Earth, in a world and in a particle.

How is government, how are these various yet similar states, to be maintained? By motive energies diversely modified in all the forces of nature. Taking one modification of force—Mechanism: it is an attribute of every entity endowed with figure and space; it is inseparable from every individual and compound—whether at rest or in motion; and is inseparable, so far as we can see, from motion itself.

The science of mechanism, as applied to the universe, is Geometry and Astronomy. By these we follow nature from the first origin—seed—egg—to the greatest dimensions: including the indefinitely large, or the indescribably small; a world in a particle, or a particle in a world.

Gaining knowledge, we try conclusions, and find the same parts and elements, but infinitely varied, in a particle and in the all-embracing heaven. There is in densest and purest substances an ætherial influx; and as if by another or similar order of æther, sensational, mental, and emotional consciousness acts along and through vibratory motions; in fact excites those volitions of which we are conscious when we put forth power.

Thus we obtain some approximate conception of influence by means of volition on matter; and, we speak reverently, of the means used in Divine operation; and of the media uniting states and places, solar vortexes and starry heavens. It is as if by study of lowly hovels we ascended to palaces of the sky; from influences, acting in earthly dust, could trace the knitting of the stupendous arch of heaven, and the rearing of magnificent courts; and knew, as by breath of Inspiration, how God, creating and ruling, studs the vast expanded dome with many stars; and in very exuberance of love enriches and beautifies our Earth.

These æthereal media, or whatever we may ultimately find them, are of various gradations as to operation. They are interior and exterior; dependent and independent; like magnetism—negative and positive; and their maintenance, if physical, is probably by atomic and molecular repulsions and attractions. For sake of definiteness, if definiteness be desirable, think of Evolution in one of its aspects—"Form." Everything is called a "thing" on account of its form, so says Aristotle. By means of the form of an entity we understand why it is of a peculiar genus or species, of one quality rather than another; consequently we may say—" The law is contained in the form;" and form is perceived by our educated sense of sight.

There are forms of other substances which are only mentally discerned in our fashioning of images abstractedly from matter. In higher sense, Form means the universe: as containing all and everything within its embrace. In highest sense, Form means God: as the One by, in, and for whom all have being and exist.

Speaking of forms generally, we say of every natural substance, it is a system of internal and external qualities. Form is built up outwardly by action from within; and, as it must stop somewhere, the different points at which it stops, as it communicates different and peculiar figures, are the limits of its evolution.

The true character of every natural and specific figure gives it not merely surface but bounds: the bounds to which the internal essence and outer environment extend —arrival at which is termination. Consequently, Form is that outward universal signature by which Nature makes herself known and limits her several productions: the obvious test by which we know this to be a vegetable, that an oak, the other an animal: the essential determination, or fluxion, or coincidence, of parts—points —substances—forces.

By cultivation we are able to raise our mind above the ideas which take form and quantity from space and time; and acquire intellectual and emotional relish for things spiritual and Divine. Every man of accurate and true intellect is able to think in a sphere above that of nature, and actually does so think—if he has been true to himself. The organic processes, so we may call them, of this mental development are exquisitely delicate. Taking the outer and mechanical basis of them, the thickness of a nerve fibre may be taken as 1,200th part of a line; central fibres are incomparably finer, and in a single square inch of the brain are packed about six millions of such fibres. By means of this mysterious organization, we pass from the fine relations and disposition of filaments, to the mental and emotional relations of spiritual activities entwining with them; until, by consummate development, we pass into secret operations which we cannot unravel: impenetrable as to physics, yet not as to our senses. These nebulæ in the sky of our intellect, which we cannot at present resolve, are indications of inner worlds and processes yet to be revealed.

Other thoughts, as to Law within the Law, can be put into more simple shape.

The Anatomist concludes that every bone found in the rocks served a purpose; and, by examination of the bone, he attains knowledge of the size, shape, food, habits of an animal which he clothes with sinews and flesh; and then depicts, so that we may see it browsing amongst the trees, ferns, reeds of an ancient world. By this fact, variously verified, we have an intimate persuasion that a chain of law, order, affinity, binds all nature together; that the essences, forms, numbers, of mental, emotional, and physical powers are united by some universal, deep, inward dependence. The moral tie binding with not less force than the physical, the religious tie holding with like restraint, man being physical, moral, religious.

Thinking of these inner and outer dependencies, we find that they crowd one upon another, and are so vast that science cannot formulate them. Our foreknowledge in some things is extensive, in others very limited. We anticipate the position of a satellite of Saturn hundreds of years hence, but cannot predict the state of our bodily health for an hour. As a rule, the things within our foresight are placed beyond our power; those within our power are beyond our foresight. Both are so co-ordinated that we know wisdom prevails in each—that events do not happen casually, but by co-operation. The skill of Swammerdam affords exquisite illustration. His minute and accurate dissections demonstrated that the future butterfly lay, with all its parts neatly folded up, in the caterpillar. It is a beautiful example of past life preparing for future life. The "Astronomical Almanac," which we draw out for years to come, rests on no firmer arrangement than does the course of the winds—which we cannot tabulate; than the cycles of human emotions—which the wise and pure may elevate to sublimity, or the low and sensual degrade to the lowest depth of natural brute appetite.

The fixity and unfixity are both modes of Divine Government. If there are free beings in the world, and doubtless there are: "How would it look to you," said King Alfred, "if there were a very powerful king, and he had no free-men in all his kingdom, but that all were slaves?" Said I—"It would not be thought by me right nor reasonable that only men in a servile condition should attend him." "Then," quoth he, "it would be more unnatural if God, in all His Kingdom, had no free creature under His power: therefore He made two rational creatures, angels and men, and gave them the great gift of freedom, with laws unto this end. Hence they could do evil and good, whichever they would." So it is: the firmest and surest of our convictions is that we can do or not do, are capable of good and evil, count for something as to our own and other's destiny. This freedom, if real, cannot be foreseen as to the whole of its conduct, otherwise freedom is not freedom.

Our reasoning is not a guessing at the half and multiplying by two; as did the Greeks in their famous philosophical question—Is the soul to the body as harmony to the harp? or as a rower to the boat? Does the soul cease—as music? or survive—as the rower, though his boat may be destroyed? We can prove that the soul is as a rower—the Greeks could not—by actual science ; that a spontaneous energy resides in the nervous centres, possessing the power of initiating molecular movements without any antecedent sensation from without ; or emotion from within ; or, so far as we can tell, from any antecedent state of feeling whatever ; or any stimulus extraneous to the moving apparatus itself. This is the essential prelude to voluntary power—the essential organic base to our unity of consciousness—the Physical Magna Charta of our freedom.

Proceed to the Verification :—

We know that we are ourselves, and not others. Every one can say—" I am I, I am not you, I am one person. I know that there is within me a co-ordinating, self-presiding power, making me one Individuality. I know as to the existence of matter, or if not of matter itself, I am conscious of those forces which manifest the so-called properties ; and I know of mind, an inner cogitating ego. Matter may be merely a dream ; but, if I find it so, I still am I. There are other minds, or intelligences, besides my own mind ; and I and these, being imperfect—therefore not self-caused—exist and have being because of Mind Supreme.

We know, then, for there is more or less of correspondence between the body and that we call the soul, between matter and mind, between physics and metaphysics ; that thinking appears to work by molecular motions in the nervous substance of the brain, and that neural tremors are connected with the key-board of the body ; yet Homer and Demosthenes, Milton and Shakespeare, you and I, are not wholly exterior ; nor do we utter a song, however the keys are set in motion, unless we ourselves have something to do with the music, and move the keys by ineffable touch.

Look into this closely. Physiologists observe two kinds of fibres in the nervous mechanism: one styled automatic arcs, the other volitional. Fix your attention on these: they are a key to the whole study of the nature of the relation between the mind of man and his muscular apparatus; between the manifestations of intelligence or intentional adaptations of means to ends, and unreasoning instinct; between the bodily man and the mental man. We must, in our thought, separate these two existences. Our body is the instrument by which our mind comes into relation with the external world. Our mind, the ego within us, means something distinct from the terrestrial world; it feels, thinks, reasons, judges, and determines—receiving all its impressions from external things through instrumentality of the body. Again—except in so far as spirit acts directly upon spirit—all the action of our ego upon the external world is by medium of the body; and thus we make mind reciprocate mind much more than the body reciprocates the body, so that "Thoughts rule the world."

The contrast between the automatic and volitional parts of the nervous system is striking. Those organisms possessing only the lower are automata. Those possessing the upper have more or less power of will, and are responsible according to the measure of that possession. Let this physical and mental fact be fully grasped. It is that which science and philosophy must further and carefully investigate. It speaks a language which has not one empty word, a language full of mystery: for sensation, thought, emotion are so utterly incongruous with physical tremors, that their connection is not seeable by the mind.

Carry the thought a little further :—We awake before opening our eyes: that is one out of thousands of proofs that external irritation is not always necessary to internal activity: it is an example of the use of power to enable us to escape from the effects of a former state. It may be otherwise illustrated :—A deep cut in the finger leaves a scar that is never obliterated; though every seven years, some say one year, the whole finger and the whole body change all their substance. It is evidence of the permanence and reality underlying all phenomena. Take a further view. Evil habits, vicious courses, the dull inebriate's life, and the vile person's seared brain, though every particle of the body and brain has passed away, are a lasting curse to the possessor; and carry the evil beyond the grave to children's children. To resist, and in part overcome this abiding evil, the volitional nerve arcs may be put into action; giving power to check and modify the automatic action of the nervous mechanism which has been abused.

The power may, by force of habit, become almost automatic—whether for good or evil. Satan's orator can acquire fluent, powerful, extemporaneous eloquence; and the pious man fall into a tendency to slovenly speech. We may sear our nervous system with evil habits, and thus scar our conscience as with a red-hot iron; or, little by little, gracefully fashion ourselves, and build up a character beautifully strong. The soul of one man wells forth as a living spring, and flows as a river of life to many. Another man, by abuse of voluntary power, becomes as one possessed by a demon. We are not to regard the action of our volitional nervous arcs as a creating of force; but, rather, as springs for the optional opening of reservoirs of energy, stored within, and given in connection with the endowment of free-will.

Experience shows that the bodily and mental constitution acquired during our period of growth becomes "a second nature," and the whole of the nervo-muscular apparatus concerned in executing the mandates of the mind acts as a trained automaton. When we mentally determine to do a thing, we will. The will does not, as physiologists formerly believed, throw itself into a particular set of muscles; but says to the automaton, "Do this," and it does it. Those who maintain that the mind is essentially and wholly dependent upon the bodily organization, would thereby exclude all possibility of real *self*-direction. John Stuart Mill, speaking of this, says—"I felt as if I was scientifically proved to be the helpless slave of antecedent circumstances, as if my character and that of all others had been formed for us by agencies beyond our control, and was wholly out of our own power." The real facts of the case are, as he himself states—"We have real power over the formation of our own character; our will, by influencing some of our circumstances, can modify our future habits or capacities of willing." We all feel that this fairly represents the real facts. In our earlier life, our characters are formed for us rather than by us; but there comes a time when we take the formation into our own hands, and thenceforth it depends mainly upon ourselves what course the development shall take. The most valuable result of early training is the enabling us to be our own masters, to keep lower appetites and passions in subjection, and to give full favourable exercise to our higher faculties.

In some measure, then, the soul or spirit, or that which puts volition in action, if not able to create force, is able to acquire energy. From what reservoir does it so acquire? Is it from the vast universe, flowing in according to the measure of the man; and from a nearness—the nearness of God Almighty? Who knows? We want the strong and wise of our race to be up and doing, to gird themselves with science, reverently to explore the mysteries, and tell us plainly concerning the energy, physical and intellectual, that we find in the world, whether or not it cometh, as we assert, from God Almighty. The question and the marvel turn not on the continuance of our own being, this seems involved in the fact that we already are in being: to die means simply that change by which we become no longer perceptible to ordinary sense. Physicists assert that a simple elementary atom is an everlasting being. We claim for the soul like permanence, and transcendental reality, akin to that which is involved in the being and existence of the world, and which survives all changes. As a man throweth away old garments and putteth on new, so the unknown energy bringeth forth and inhabiteth the new. Even the atoms are energized by Intelligence—the Cause of all causation—the Life of all that lives—the Mind of all that thinks.

Now view the mental training, or process, by which energy may be acquired so as to give highest development to our character.

We are all able determinately to fix our attention upon some one object. We can look upon a picture, then examine every part separately. We can, if we have a musical ear, single out any instrument in an orchestra and follow it through the whole performance. Carry this fact to any object of study, endeavour to fix and maintain your attention by sufficient effort. That determinate effort is an act of the will, and the power of so fixing and concentrating attention is almost the highest and best in our intellectual self-education, and is the great means by which we effect our moral self-improvement. This selective attention, intensifying of mental gaze; then making the object fixed on call up some other, and another, until knowledge, or memory, by determinate fixation, attains the desired result; is the secret of high moral and mental success. Every child should be taught to do this. Begin with a few minutes at a time; by gradual and judicious training the child will gladly exert itself determinately; and thus will be laid that foundation without which nothing supremely good can be attained, whether in intellectual study or in moral discipline.

Look at the moral side. We may be tempted to indulge in wine, to apply our powers to ill uses, to play some mean trick, to gain credit not due to us. Though we cannot bring motives before our mind, can only take what comes to our mind, we can think of the wrong, of the consequences, and determinately direct our attention, our conscience, to the reasons why we should not do the evil thing; and we can fix our attention upon something else. Dr. W. B. Carpenter says—" I ask you to take as your guiding star, as it were, in the conduct of your lives, these four words—'I am, I ought, I can, I will.' 'I am,' is the expression of reflection and self-consciousness, the looking in upon our own trains of thought. 'I ought,' expresses the sense of moral obligation—Turn to the right, and keep straight on. 'I can'—the consciousness of power—is the foundation of all effort. Lastly, it is not enough to say, 'I am, I ought, I can'—we must *will* to do it. 'I will,' of the ego, can train the mental as well as the bodily of the Automaton, and make it do anything it is capable of executing." In still higher sense, we use the freedom wherewith Christ hath made us free.

Thus our wonderful nervous mechanism renders us able to regard our Earth as holy ground, and gives an illumination that causes the universe to shine with light as of the sacred bush. We find the place of faculties, and discover that the frontal lobes of our brain are the principal seat of intellect. We know, as scientific thinkers, that within certain limits of choice and action, we are free from compulsion of the vital, social, and dynamical forces at work in the cosmos. We know, as moral beings, that we are accountable, within a sphere of which our consciences are sufficiently informed, for the use of our faculties of thought, of emotion, of action.

Thus our mind, our soul, our spirit, leads forth the army of its power; the action of the volitional nervous mechanism is not wholly originated, nor performed by —may, indeed, be independent of—the physical causes which operate in the automatic nervous arcs. The will continually initiates movements: is that reality, fact, and force, present in our consciousness, which is a greater certainty than any other certainty. The distinction between voluntary and involuntary movement is recognized by every physiologist. The spirit of life is not the mechanism, nor its motion; but that which makes, that which moves it—a law within the law. That which so lived as to build the mechanism may survive the unbuilding, sing a song more wonderful, tell a tale more marvellous, than any sung or said in our present habitation.

This Power of Volition, of Law Within the Law, of Freedom, of Responsibility, of Future Life, demands that provision be made by the Supreme for every event, an arrangement by the Infinite which takes into account all the actuals and possibles, so that no creature—however small, no event—however trifling, is or can be out of control.

When possible evil becomes actual, the interposition of remedy; of narrowing, or of enlargement; of death, or of life; are not brought in by a change of the Eternal's laws, but by operation of law within the law. He does not recall the fire of Etna when a saint is near, nor impress earth or sea with new motions that gravitation may cease because a pious man is nigh. Through action of other powers, other agencies, ordained from the beginning, comes warning or punishment, restraint or relief; and, it may be, help from a profundity that seemed before but shallowness. Can our understanding comprehend, or conceive of anything more enlarged than this dealing of an omnipresent God? Can our wisdom find more profound occupation than the searching such depths of Divine Counsel? Can our imagination ascend higher than this throne of

Divinity? The reason, Divine reason, enabling us so to think, constitutes our essential superiority to all other earthly creatures. By it we are foreseeing, versatile, acute, and have such wonderful memory. By it we are made, so Cicero said, "an excerpt from the Divine;" and by it, so Seneca said, "the spirit of man is a portion, as it were spark of the Divine Spirit." To speak of God as spirable, or of man as inspirable, is only of course to say—"He has endowed us with a mind which faintly reflects His own." By this mind we seek Him, know Him, and are enabled, in some degree, to hold converse with Him, love Him, serve Him. No man was ever truly great without an inspiration from on high, and no poet worth the name who was not inflamed by Divine truth.

The half-learned man laughs at the simple faith which believes that rain comes from God; but the philosopher arrives at the conclusion that God is seen in the rain and the sunshine, in the great and the small. The true cure for half-learning is thorough learning: that Divine Government is leading all things to new manifestations of goodness, though life's storms drive towards a rocky shore. Why do these storms rage? Because evil abounds? "Here is sin," says a voice from one quarter; "Here is sin," repeats a voice from another quarter; everything finds speech to declare—"Sin and guilt are here." How great, then, the need for skilful arrangement, that those who have broken loose from moral restraint shall not be bound with physical chains to enforced obedience; but, won by love, be gently restrained by sense of right! It is Wisdom's highest operation when, by Law Within the Law, the turns and winds of human life, and all evil in the world, are guided by winsome purity—are assuaged by gentle persuasiveness of righteousness—so that Wisdom and Law never fail. Wisdom and Law so binding nature to the Supernatural, that every evil is made the procuring cause of greater good; and not the unusual only, but every common event, is adorned with a halo of the miraculous; and every miracle is a star within nature's sky.

THOUGHT XXIII.

EVOLUTION AS A TRUE THEORY.

"Even the poorest aspect of Nature, especially of living Nature, is a type and manifestation of the Invisible Spirit that works in Nature . . .
He is wise who discerns Wisdom in unpretending forms, and recognizes Her royal features under week-day vesture . . . Late in man's history, but clearly it becomes manifest that Mind is stronger than matter, that Mind is the Creator and Shaper of matter."—THOMAS CARLYLE.

THEOLOGIANS do not object to the theory of Evolution. They know that the Divine account of Creation, expressive of orderly development, reveals a most wonderful process of Evolution. It is the materialistic, atheistic abuse against which all religious people protest. The blow-hole of a shark may be the prototype of a human ear, and the science of Embryology indicate that the rudimentary forms of a man represent the fashions of his forefathers; while a very curious African Toad is the very earliest existing being that possessed toe and finger-nails like those of a human being. Suppose then we say—that men ascended from worms, fishes, reptiles? Does it not seem reasonable to hold that the physical unity of the universe is proof of plan, and that the variety is a lasting universal proof of wonderful energy everywhere unfolding in a vast cosmical miracle?

We offer a germ of thought concerning the universal application of evolution as a means whereby the Almighty worked, and continues to work, manifold processes.

The Universe presents many Aspects. The Supernatural and Natural, the Miraculous and Common, the Idealistic and Materialistic.

The Supernatural, Miraculous, Idealistic, are thought of as the modes in which the Supreme transcends all finite intelligence; not only in the ascertained laws of the universe, but also in His own Nature with regard to time—space—sensation.

The Materialist discerns merely the Natural and Common—not even the brighter features in them: does not seem to grasp the true meaning and reality of anything beyond the space-filling stuff of the universe; though, indeed, he only knows even of this matter by means of its resistance to imagination and will; and, in refusing to allow that there is an Intelligent Author, reduces the cosmos to an organism destitute of life. He does not see, well and lovingly, the solemn vistas ever opening into infinitude; is rather the victim of mechanical art than the subject of inspiration; and, far from discerning new beauties day by day, deifies brute Force as were matter the iron mask of a formless, powerless Eternity.

We confess that the great difficulty for those who believe in Infinite Power and Goodness is to reconcile these with the known facts of the world. Most men, however, unduly magnify the difficulty: for as we acknowledge our own individual nature—physical, intellectual, moral—to have been developed from a small

Evolution as a True Theory.

beginning; there ought to be nothing insuperable against the hypothesis that the cosmos is also progressive, with parts enigmatical as in our own life, with rudimentary processes, and with provision for every kind of intelligence, so that all may finally attain maturity and glorious state. Thus viewed, the weaknesses and anomalies of the world present a proof of design; and, as for the world-wonders, they clearly stand as heavenly signs.

If any quibble at the word design, they may say "purpose." Now, as to this purpose, thus think of it. There cannot be progression without a past, a present, a future. The past is as an indefinitely extended line in one direction, the future as an indefinitely extended line in another direction, the present we may call an intersecting line; or that in which, so far as our life now is concerned, the past and future meet. Now add the conception that this infinitely extended line rotates from left to right. Then reason further—the progress from infinity to infinity is actual; and not only as in a line, but for production of things and existences, there must be a convergence of the infinite circumference into the individual. Thus, the purpose effectuated in the existence of a responsible—that is, an intellectual and moral being, is not only united to an immeasurable past; but gives to that being relations onwards and upwards, connects it with a real spiritual unseen Infinity, and endows it with the possibility of eternity; that is, the capacity of immortality.

This conception of a spiritual unseen bearing down upon us from an infinitude—having relations with a past and a future eternity, enables us scientifically to account for our consciousness of God; and the possibility of immortality affords not only a plea for Revelation, but qualifies us to attain conception concerning the unity of life and intelligence: a vital and intellectual binding together corresponding to the strong mechanical physical bond which we can scientifically perceive. The realities here may seem, to those defective in spiritual insight, pale, thin, and ineffectual as Ossian's ghosts; but unto the possessors of adequate power to delineate the wants and aspirations of spiritual nature they will be as the light of stars, shining through everything; so that the embodied actualities of human nature, the hitherto unwrought potentialities, all the exquisite scenes of natural beauty—where no man comes or hath come since the making of the world, become not mere shows of possibilities, but real prophetic tokens of immortality, Heavenly signs of God acting as a wise Father, and revealing sources of joy to many spiritual intelligences.

Thus able, as we are, from our thought of time and eternity, of space and infinitude, and of progress in nature, to evolve a persuasion of the Divine Existence, and a conviction of immortality; it is clear that the Supernatural, Miraculous, and Idealistic, are not inconsistent with the Natural, the Common, the Materialistic —otherwise, our faculties would be in permanent confusion, which is absurd. Indeed, we are compelled to believe in an all-pervading conscious existence; we naturally associate even the motions of matter with some occult sensation—a life escaping our observation. This finite conception of Godhead, even as the interpretation of Revelation, and the teachings by scientific men, must necessarily be imperfect; and it is owing to forgetfulness of this that the merely mechanical of scientific men, and the merely theoretic of theologians, separate into two hostile camps.

If, then, we discern that the natural and the revealed are not separated by any hard and fast line; if we perceive that all limited and conditioned things are connected with infinitude and eternity; that the visible universe was formed by an Intelligence residing in the unseen; so that our knowledge of God and persuasion of immortality, though partaking of the Supernatural and miraculous, are truly scientific; we may inquire concerning that matter, or space-filling stuff, of which things are formed.

Is Matter eternal? Investigation must precede reply.

We are making wonderful advance in discovering the physical unity of the cosmos; we find that the great masses of the universe are bound together by a bond scientifically perceived, and that they appear to be made of the same materials. We think that we know somewhat of the origin, growth, and decay of worlds. The human race must perish; the earth, sun, planets, all other suns and planets, pass away; but the terrific crash may be followed by origination of new worlds in an endless recurring series, say, if you will—with ever increasing splendour. Does the assertion seem probable, that amidst this universal decay and rejuvenescence of worlds the atoms, of which they are composed, must be regarded as eternal? If we cannot regard the sun, with its vast store of forces, as eternal; is it reasonable that the individual atoms, with such comparatively infinitesimal small store of energy, should be everlasting? Take a general scientific opinion—" The primordial atoms were all of the same pattern, of intensely rapid vibration, and always in motion; differences were formed by various groupings, and hence we have those we call elements." Consequently, we must look upon these atoms as collocations of energy in space; they are structures even more complicate than a watch—considered merely as a watch; they are only less complex than a whole universe; therefore, we are irresistibly and naturally led to think of some anterior state, an unseen universe, out of which the existing atoms were brought.

If thus brought forth, by what, or by whom, was the process wrought? Could it have been by means of vortex-motion set up in the æther, or in some other fluid filling the whole of space? This fluid could hardly have, of itself, a natural propensity to develop vortex-rings; so we must presume there was a prior universe, and like or unlike that of the æther from which the present has been derived; and that, too, must have been developed from a previous state; so there has been process after process, forming together a vista of worlds of which it is impossible to see the end; yet, as there must have been origination or beginning wherever succession exists, these many worlds, however far traced back, were evolved by action of the Deity in bringing forth the elements, and in giving them finished structure.

We must also regard the phenomena of life as developed from the unseen; and these, with the objective realities, are but as a small fringe of that Divine garment—the Universe; therefore, the development was not a dead development. Even a tiny crystal, placed in "a saturated solution" of the same salt, multiplies copies of itself. Hence we see that there is a subjective and life-side: atoms in nowise suggest a dead process. There is, at the least, probability that in the universe many groups would be formed so as to develop into that life and consciousness, and individual complexity, which we now recognize. They were structures of more skill, marvellous motion, and complex power, than a watch; and their being all alike—if they were alike—and their enormously great number, lead us to conclude that they were not by unintelligent fortuity, but by Intelligence purposing uniformity.

Not only so, biologists affirm that no organized being can be produced except from an organized antecedent. This we must take account of, and hold that life can only spring from life; for we must, if men are to agree at all, take the universe to be as it is known. This hypothesis of the evolution of life from life, leads to the recognition of previous life in a precedent world, of an intelligent living Unseen. The life of our globe, like the life of every individual, descended to it; and as we go back and back, we come at length to one Life—one Being—one God, who has developed and sustains the present order.

All is natural, all is supernatural, and every phenomenon is a revelation. One particular body of knowledge, the ordinary working of the universe, we call—"science." Another particular body of knowledge, we call—"the prophets' book," yielding desirable information, not derivable from nature's common process. This better knowledge has great practical usefulness, placing the possessors in a position of advantage. It gives them a religious conviction of immortality; in virtue of which they are full of generous and noble faith, feel that they can achieve excellence; and by means—even of things most disastrous, and in positions—otherwise hopeless and helpless, work out a glorious, physical, vital, mental, and moral condition. This must at length drive out that poor shallow view that the universe is only bound together by physical force.

The best men are agreed that it is altogether outrageous to speak of the Christian Revelation as if it were a mere dogma of one of the many schools of human philosophy. They know that the mysteries involved in the Incarnation, the Life, the Death, the Resurrection of the Founder of our Faith, cannot even now be perfectly understood. Human intellects are very limited, we must act on the evidence of faith, and not alone on the evidence of our senses. We differ in the widest possible manner on all questions of the day —whether in politics or science—can we expect to have the means of *fully* judging concerning matters of faith, seeing that reason itself is not able in full strength to help? The Bible was, from the beginning, a progressive and continuous revelation culminating in Christianity. It is now, as by spiritual evolution in a Divine sense, culminating in the glory of our race and habitation. We, in obedience to the higher principles of our nature, believe in spiritual presences—such as the angels; and in spiritual energies conducting men to the exquisite scenes and life of the future. If, on the contrary, there could be a nation in utter disbelief as to a future state and responsibility to God, that nation would in consequence lose power, and at once begin to fall to pieces.

The wonderful realities—God, Immortality, Revelation, are in connection with a system, infinitely vast, of teleological development, with truths very early established, the height and depth of which we are only beginning to apprehend. Regarded merely as the evolved intellectual and emotional conviction that men are responsible to the Supreme; and, as such, the great motive power in duty, the great consoler in trouble, the great enabler to excellence; it is in the highest sense unreasonable and unscientific to allow the materialization of a few peculiarly—not excellently constituted minds, to excite doubt concerning realities so supremely great and good. Not only the life of Christ, the lives of all holy men are proof of the truth of Christianity; and we regard the Decalogue, more than three thousand years old, as a wonderful product. Our Saviour, viewed even as a mere man, did more for ethics than ten men like Newton could do for physics. Now for ages, little has been done by any or all the men in the world, except the practical application to life of the Divine Doctrines long ago given. How unwise to put physical science always, until of late, in a backward state—in antagonism to spiritual and moral truth. Nature is not a hindering restraint to freedom, it is the organ of freedom; and as the miraculous element reveals the unity of spirit and of nature, that element anticipates and predicts a state of harmony and beauty for which the present is a teleological transition period. We are everywhere surrounded by invisible supernatural sacred influences acting on nature—preparing for greater things.

When these great things are done, we shall know what the Bible really is, that Inspiration means much more than we thought, that the whole world, all the arts of life, every science, and even Death itself, perform parts in our spiritual education.

We count many things evil, there are perplexing occurrences and things out of joint, but to the Great Governor they doubtless present a different aspect. Disease and accident are messengers by whom He summons men to His presence; while marvel and miracle, enigma and parable, proving the dependence of nature on the Creator, are means of awakening and strengthening intelligence and faith. Miracles have not ceased, but are rare in these days, because the Incarnation of Christ and the Presence of the Holy Spirit are permanent miracles. As time goes on, the Holy Spirit will enable the willing to possess and manifest the true essence of Christianity. Even now, we assert, a standing miracle exists and has always existed—a direct continual influence of the Supernatural on the natural. The truly faithful are assisted and guided every instant. Had every precaution been taken, apart from our own will, so that physical nature of itself had always every degree and kind of guiding and driving power, conscience would have been an absurd, therefore, impossible thing. Now, if you would lose gloom and wretchedness, look within the veil.

Some of the Old Testament miracles were adapted to the primitive state; and their peculiarity, rightly regarded, conveys speciality of evidence as to truth. They live on in that which they confirmed; and that, of itself, is a miracle, for Bible Truth is most aggressive.

Men fed on it are instinct with enterprise, no old-world fixity is in them, no one thinks exactly the same thing, everywhere is expansiveness. Our Christian faith, or religious system, is never in a state of indolent repose. Though rising in the East, it has not Oriental fixity, the everlasting *status quo;* it is ever acting, fighting, and fought against. Ever and ever is some Reformation, and this will go on, making the old Revelation new, until men have arrived at an adequate conception of the true meaning, power, and essence of Christianity.

This may be called a materialization of spiritual processes, doubtless, and when psychology is developed as a branch of knowledge, we shall see many glories in the light of day. Meanwhile, when rare phenomena are observed, anything not falling in with our preconceived opinions, we must learn to have faith. Swedenborg was neither a deceiver nor mad; by clairvoyance he saw and described the progress of a fire in a distant city. We do not sufficiently cultivate that power by which we read and influence the mind of another, by action from a distance, without any visible means. In all this, formal science may enlarge its borders, and obtain knowledge of other intelligent residents in the universe. The best does not always spread fastest in natural selection; therefore, the Supernatural comes in. There are virtually in us the rudiments of the highest and noblest; but it is only as they are evolved by faith, painstaking, prayer, and obedience, that we become high and noble. What good and evil lie in that fact! Doubtless, the day is coming when men, not leaving uncultivated the finer elements of spiritual life, shall find new harmonies and an improved understanding; a sunny firmament will be within their inner world; they will have communion not only with the low but the high of this wonderful universe; the present faint prospects and far-off indications waxing into present and possessed glory; so that they live with their whole being. Fulness of Christianity is fulness of the laws of the world.

THOUGHT XXIV.

LIGHT OF NATURE.

"In tantum videbimus Deum, in quantum sumus similes."

EVERY blade of grass in our green flowery well-built earth is a manifestation of unknown power, whose essence and life reside in the Eternal—much more wonderful is man.

Quackery and dupery have been busy among us, babbling poorly, with sounding nomenclature, physical experimenting, and what not, to prove—that God everywhere is not God With Us. Common sense is now awaking, and thinks—"Mind makes the man, and the soul stamps him as of worth." Mind carries man to see the reason of matter's thousand-fold complexity of forces; and mind discerns that Intelligence cannot be darkest where thought shines brightest. Mind says—"If God reveals His thoughts in the stars, which cannot know anything, is it not that men may be instructed? Is it not to brighten the courts of science, and halls of literature?" We certainly have a revelation in the stars of Eternal Power and Godhead, we certainly possess God-consciousness. These two are, in a sense, incarnation and inspiration; so that the greater Incarnation—God in Christ, and the greater Inspiration—God in the Word—

Holy Scripture, well comport themselves with our sacred persuasion that the true man is a pavilion of Deity, and that our intellect and emotion are candles lighted by the Lord.

God has endowed man with attributes that we know are not matter, even as light, heat, gravity are not matter, but transformers of matter; something by which he rises above material nature, subdues its laws, and possesses a human supernatural as if in token of the Divine Supernatural.

Materialists attribute to matter all the properties usually counted spiritual; drag things invisible and heavenly down to earth, not to advance our knowledge, for they declare that nothing is real but what we strike against and touch, forgetting that these properties prove that energy has entered matter; the entrance showing that it was aforetime apart from it. Now if energy enters matter, and constructs the worlds by atomic and molecular arrangement, using very little atomic, and some microscopic living workers; of whom twenty-seven millions and more may live and labour within an inch of space; are we to account their insignificance the cause of all the worlds' magnificence? Is man, who finds that every human handy-work is graven with man's device, to say that the skilled work of the universe was wrought without skill; and that all the intelligence comes from those little labourers who have no mind nor will? Certainly not. The universe is a vast visible embodied plan. Nor is that all: vegetable life contains, so to speak, a soul in the bud; animal life, *anima bruti*, is the soul looking out of the windows of sense; in man there is a sparkling and glitter of intelligence—a very lamp of God. We shall never cease to believe that the body of man—understood in the highest sense—is a Divine incarnation; and that the spirit is so advanced beyond all other things that it is, pre-eminently, a shadow of the Holy Ghost.

This blessed Light of Nature enlightening us so that, by retrospection, we trace the past; and, by foreknowledge, possess the future; is, in itself, a guarantee that we shall not go darkling down to death eternal. The vast tide of human will, emotion, intelligence, and God-consciousness, so overflows the material margin of our earthly existence, that even while in the flesh we possess knowledge and assurance concerning a Diviner Kingdom. Refusing the error of attempting to grind the sacred mysteries of religion, and the noblest sentiments of human nature, out of the habits and instincts of lowest animals, we accept the saying of Seneca—"Quid aliud vocas animam quàm Deum in humano corpore hospitantem?" What less can you call the soul than God condescending to dwell in a house of clay? Those who think that the genius of great men can be chemically explained by productions within or outside Leyden jars, or as a result of phosphorus, ought to consider the ancient moralist's words—"Ratio nil aliud est quam in corpus humanum pars Divini Spiritûs mersa"—Reason is somewhat of a Divinity steeped in flesh. They will do well to remember that mind, viewed even in very low scientific sense, cannot be handled and dealt with as a palpable object. The molecular, chemical, vital processes of the nervous elements of the brain are not a material jumble; but a going forth from some mysterious source inspiring and moving organic growth throughout the Earth, generating man's highest energy and bestowing genius. Lord Bacon well observes—"The soul of man was not produced by heaven or earth, but was breathed in immediately from God: so that the ways and proceedings of God with spirits are not included in nature; that is in the laws of heaven and earth, but are reserved to the laws of His secret will and grace."

The spirit is the life of our spiritual or resurrection body (1 Cor. xv. 44). The spirit is that principle by which we contemplate God: and as in virtue of the æther that fills all space and pervades all matter, we behold remotest stars and measure astronomical distance by comparing angles, so that all things in the starry system appear as if they were present; in like manner, by medium of the spirit, we recall the past, anticipate the future, and make the two into one now.

At present we possess this peculiar endowment subject to the narrowness limiting human minds: we have great variety of ideas only by succession. No man is able to hold together all his knowledge, and set it constantly before him in one picture. Even those with prodigy of parts and of wonderful memory, like Pascal, though they have a whole handful of truth can open only a finger: but it is certain that our present corporeal organization, which seems but a transient appendage to our spiritual humanity, possesses optical, auditory, and other nerves, which are not fully nor perfectly used. These seem premonitions of powers not yet possessed, but sure to come unless nature works in vain; manifestations of probability that our capacities of knowledge may become so extensive, that we can behold the whole Christian Dispensation in such analogy and conformity with other parts of God's world, that it shall seem not less natural than the visible and material known course now appears; the spiritual body appear natural as the material body; and the building up of the inner man, by the spirit, seem analogous to the principle of growth which now constructs the outer man.

This principle of growth, if we regard the whole man, inner and outer, the mental and material substance, will be found of more complicate character than is mere material growth; and an exception sometimes to each order of things, taken separately, but in accurate keeping with both taken together; and establishing a relation within nature. Relation by means of natural intelligence soaring into transcendent heights to possess whatever that intelligence discerns. That soaring may sometimes obtain conceptions of the Supernatural, and the relation will be real; even material, in some respects, according to materialistic doctrine: for as it is impossible, in naturals, to create a grain of sand; it is equally impossible to create a thought of spirituals if no spirituals exist. We must lay aside the silly notion that there are mental miracles, though physical are impossible; and take the common sense fact—the universal conviction that something exists beyond, above, and containing nature, is of weight equal to the other fact, that the visible world is framed of material substance.

This high illumination of intelligence throws light on nature, proves man to be a citizen of two cities; exhibits him in a natural and supernatural relationship; subjects him to the laws of matter and to the laws of mind;

enables him to act by each on both; and, more or less, in conception to separate himself from and control either. He is enabled to comprehend that he occupies a place of trial, passes through a series of temptations, not known to any other earthly creature, in order that he may become a type of faithfulness to God; and that every volition of right may combine to resist the whole power of evil.

In some respects, he is like one of those meteoric stones coming from other and distant realms to enter our world. In some respects, he is like one temporarily imprisoned within a seven-walled kingdom of darkness, that he may be an example and a proof how voluntary use of Divinely given grace obtains spiritual and natural freedom. In some respects, his spirit may be likened to an embodiment of personality formed of some sublime transcendent medium, knitting it to the infinite eternal Existence.

He has peculiarity of position with duality of nature, and from the Earth's standpoint dominates the universe. The present certainly possessing potentiality of future possession: for nothing exists in vain. The whole universe being one vast arch in which all worlds and all things are knit together to form a majestic whole, resting on the pillars of Divine Wisdom and Might.

The mystery is not utterly dark, nor is solution waited for in vain—a linked purpose unites the whole. Every particle of matter has outer form and inner substance, external and internal media, joining it to this world, linking it to all other worlds, and to every kind of existence: so that, in a sense, while on the earth, it climbs the skies; in a sense, the very commonest stuff of the universe possesses body and soul. Nor is that all: take any physical substance and fact, say fire and water with combustion: water quenches fire, yet water is essentially fiery; and each from each may be extracted. They may be life, or they may be death, to one another; apart, or in union, they are solvents of one another and all other; may be said by action, interaction, and joint action, to control seasons, change existences, rule and suspend laws — even gravity; although most amenable to law. Likewise, man, by means of body and mind, is subject to law; but can rise above it. He has a power of self-differentiation, inherent in his very nature, and can develop himself by divergencies. As chemical union changes the nature of constituents, the more mysterious union of matter and mind in man forms that amalgam which, physical process proving it possible, will effect such transformations in matter, elevation of laws, and resurrections from the dead, as render the miracles of Christ small, He Himself testifying, in comparison with those hereafter to be wrought.

Thus, miracles are master-works, a light of nature, prophecies of a glorious Humanity. In their actuality, resting on nature; in their essentiality, resting on that which, out of and apart from nature, pervades nature. On one side, they seem anomalies; on the other, they are enterings of new powers to enlarge mental capacities and material forces. They are operations somewhat akin, or analogous, to those which long ago elevated formless matter into crystals, the dead into life, and to life gave intelligence. A kind of free-will greeting the earth, and dwelling in man, as proof of independence. A signature of the Almighty, by which He owns them as His; yet restrains them, lest men regard them as ordained by Fate rather than by Intelligence.

Only those men whose reason has been somewhat narrowed by limitation to physical processes, refuse these facts. Men of highest culture, who are moulded into completeness by intellectual and emotional activity, discern that present evil and seeming waste will be turned to good and use. To them the earth is not a rubbish-heap thrown upon marshy land. Their faith is not kindled by fiery terror of brimstone-lake, a light of Lucifer; it is an illumination, as by smile of God, and grows into brightness of assured and peculiar glory. It will never sink into ineffectuality, or darksome gloom, nor die down in the wreck of many worlds; it is a far-extending ray coming out from wonderful regions to enlighten intelligence as to the Ways of Providence and Love of God.

THOUGHT XXV.

THE GOD-MAN.

> " Thou seemest human and Divine,
>   The highest, holiest Manhood, Thou :
>   Our wills are ours, we know not how ;
>   Our wills are ours, to make them Thine."
>   *In Memoriam.*

CARLYLE says—" As I take it, Universal History, the history of what man has accomplished in this world, is at bottom the history of the Great Men who have worked here. They were the leaders of men, these great ones; the modellers, patterns, and in a wide sense creators. . . This is an age that as it were denies the existence of great men; denies the desirableness of great men. Show our critics a great man, Luther for example, they begin to do what they call account for him ; not to worship him, but to take the dimensions of him,—and bring him out to be a little kind of man." Melancholy work, false work, dead work is this, done by the make-believe sort of men ; who, not kindled lamps themselves, would have us think that neither by God's gift, nor by any other's gift, do we have moral and spiritual luminaries shining by the light of Heaven.

Great men are real, grand in themselves—not creatures of circumstances, but more frequently makers of opportunity. Poets in splendour of imagination, pouring forth sparkling words overflowing with passionate beauty, give to the commonest things of life gorgeous array and divinity of inspiration. The truly great are profitable company, we can hardly look upon them—certainly not be with them without gaining something from them. Even a sentence of rhythm and melody, musically worded, possesses something deep and good in the meaning; much more a life which can greatly dare and nobly die, in which body and soul, language and idea, are gracefully linked in truth and power.

The Great Man is a force in nature which subdues and transcends nature. He establishes in earliest times a perfection not exceeded by modern progress. For power, for highest reach and widest range of mental and spiritual capacity, the ancients have not even yet been surpassed. Which sculptor excels Phidias? Æschylus, Homer, the writer of the book of Job, soar as high as any genius of our own day. David and Isaiah in sacred pathos, gentleness yet force, simplicity and sublimity, transcend all divines of present culture. As instruments of thought the Greeks were almost perfect. Exceptional greatness contains depth and height—not mechanically explainable; the genesis is unseen, and when devout always spiritual; thought and emotion modifying the outward and material. Such a man always lays to heart his duty and vital relations in this mysterious universe; the manner in which he is, or feels himself to be, spiritually related to the unseen world; and he uses life, in all its faculties, as a contribution towards making some highway to that unseen. He is no sceptic: for, whatever be the intellectual doubts;

moral doubts and insincerity, the black malady and life-foe of every age, have no place in him. Faith makes him brave in the battle-field, sustains him at the stake, and bears him up though the martyrdom be long and weary as the whole of a saddened life.

Those who see nothing but dead mechanism in the universe — checks, balances, cranks, levers; whose "Doctrine of Motives," however much disguised, gives wretched love of pleasure, or fear of pain, hunger for applause, money, or whatever it may be, as the great factors of human life, are never great. All they can manage to believe in is what they can measure and weigh, eat and digest, or clothe themselves withal: lower can no man go, and yet remain rational: to possess no God, not even a devil! It is the mournfulest and meanest of all conditions; it renders life a base creeping toward a hopeless future; it makes all talk about virtue and high motive a poor sentimental vapouring—plausible quackery. No such scantily furnished, spiritually paralytic man, is a hero. To the hero the world is instinct with Godhead, and life is the seed-time of eternity.

Even the best of sceptics is incomplete. We all feel that a man of mere intellect, however great and powerful that intellect, is inharmoniously developed: the gentler and tenderer affections are starved and chilled in him. He is as a man who keeps his spirit, as was said of Humboldt, "within an iron safe." He seems to adopt as maxim—"Il faut penser, il ne faut pas croire"—"the greater the knowledge the greater the doubt." It is really doubtful whether any such man would count any opinion certain enough, any truth sure and good enough, to be worth dying for. Find a man of mere intellect who does not assert that the noble army of martyrs greatly blundered, and that man has already added pure emotion to his intellect, he begins to be spiritually minded.

As for God, unto whom the thoughts of all spiritually minded men soar, we must conclude that He possesses, as Leibnitz says—"The qualities of a good governor, as of a great architect;" and the point of connection at which Divine Power comes into contact and government with the chain of natural causation may be the first link, running thence, as fine electrical influence, through every link and every part of a link. In any case, there was, is, and must be, an ever-abiding union by which all natural phenomena are sustained by the unseen Power. This Power, establishing ordinary agency, is still more the source of extraordinary; a great man is extraordinary, and consequently a God-man. He will give up his whole life for the welfare and improvement of other men: even as God, who spent ages in fitting the earth to be a dwelling for men, will spend ages more in fitting perfect men for a renovated earth.

He, the great and good man, represents in nature something that has no inherent limit by nature: for he greatly rules nature, and has a more intimate relation with the unseen world than other men possess. To the simple-minded he was, of old, as a god: they believed that he was near to, if not a part of Divinity. To the scientific mind of our day, he is a genius; and in the unfolding of his mind toward Divinity, a prophet; otherwise, he may be statesman, poet, artist; or world-mover by means of eloquence or arms. There is a sort of universal conviction, that as every ray of light is a child of the sun, every dew-drop a model of the ocean; so the smile of human intelligence is a mystic gleam, which in the mind and countenance of a great man shines as Divine illumination.

Highest and purest greatness displays self-sacrifice: self-sacrifice—not a degrading of the higher for elimination of imperfections from the lower; but for multiplying of graces and virtues—by taking away the selfish base from character—by infusing free and noble capacity of love—which affords grandest stimulus to high natures by enabling them to rescue the perishing. The sense of the necessity of self-sacrifice arises also from the conviction of sin and dread of punishment. The dread itself, desire of pardon, and yearning for holiness, being regarded as a premonition, and already a partial possession of immortality. These natural emotions, natural because so common, are the basis of all true religion; are promptings that lead to faith in some Redemption; establish the intellectual and moral conviction of a Divine Kingdom and King; and they can never be effaced from the human mind. This King, thus having representatives in all great men as if He lived in their flesh, became personally manifest and incarnate in the Lord Jesus Christ.

The law of self-sacrifice, the law of the Cross, received highest embodiment in Him, even Jesus, "the Form of God;" who became a servant that He might raise inferior beings to His own level, give them of His own life, of His own spirit, and by supernatural selection enable them to lay hold on eternal life. Very few of us understand the mystery and true power of self-denial, or have faith in the power of self-sacrifice. Natural selection would extinguish the feeble, blighted, maimed forms of life—by crushing them out. Christ tells us that every act of wise self-sacrifice for the weak and the miserable, is a transfer from our strength, wealth, and happiness,—is a breathing of our life, our love, our spirit, into the feeble and low, to make them partake of the Divine law of Supernatural Selection; by which the poor, the meek, the gentle, the pure in heart, are saved, raised, strengthened, that they may see God. Self-denial by the rich is not only the best means that we can use for the prevention and cure of misery; but the most efficient and, probably, an absolutely necessary instrument for raising our whole race to the highest attainable perfection.

It is a great mystery, nevertheless, in accordance with pure reason and the high consciousness of our race, that the Everlasting should give Divinity to self-denial,—manifest Himself in our flesh—be a Divine Humanity; as if to prove that the great and pure hero is a God-like man. The Incarnation affirms the twofold truth of universal consciousness, that in some way exceedingly beneficial to us, God is like man, and the true man is like God. It is now nearly two thousand years since the actual historic manifestation; but the miracle, though more fully believed in, is rather greater than less in wonder. We are more capable of discernment as to the reality: for now, that scientifically we regard the universe as a whole, we see that it is also, in every atom, that material garment with which the Eternal clothes His energy; even as in all the intelligence of creatures, in all genius—science—art—literature—design, are manifestations of the Supreme Mind. We discern somewhat more clearly than did our forefathers, that human nature, as conscious of God, is in itself an incarnation; grandly, beautifully, sacredly, summed up in Christ Jesus. Thus the three great Revelations of God in the World, in Literature, in Flesh, stand plainly before us in Creation, in Scripture, in Christ.

Time did not call Christ forth, nor was He the creature of circumstance: Time often calls loudly for great men, but there are none to answer; and Circumstance often diminishes the great one, and makes him like the many small. If Time and Circumstance could always discern and find a great man, Time and Circumstance need never go to ruin.

Moreover—Jesus, the God-man, was not an evolution; unless by an unfathomable law of like producing unlike. This may be proved: great men, the inventors of useful arts, prophets, poets, do not, as a rule, produce extraordinary children; nor create great breaks, nor cause surprising leaps in the intellect of mankind; they rather exhaust the honoured family. It is consequently found that great men, more frequently than otherwise, are not children of the great. Atavism, meaning the occasional reappearance of rare forms and powers, does not explain—it only states the fact. Without any adequate assignable cause, great men appear by an interruption, a suspension, or an elevation of our nature. The earth may not tremble at the birth of a gifted infant, nor the face of heaven shine with fiery portents, but a mighty thing has happened, and the mystery— a work of Providence—presents an enigma to science.

As to Christ Himself, the fact must also be otherwise stated: He, the ideal, the perfection of our race, appeared in an age when such an ideal could not have been developed in act—could not have been conceived of in thought. In the Theory of Development, the perfection of humanity is the final result of man's history ages hence; Christ, therefore, is the one great miracle which more than any other establishes the fact of miracles. Christ is Himself the proof of His own miracles.

Jesus is not only mysterious, as are the greatest of our race; He seems, from the fact that none before were like Him, to have marched over the dead and living bodies of all our race to a marvellous material, spiritual, and moral victory. In Him were the noblest principles of greatness exalted to sublimity, and the profoundest depths of misery were fathomed by personal suffering and true sympathy. He was a man of sorrow—yet the Son of God, He was the Holy—yet dealt with us impure. He was the union of absolute grandeur and helpless lowliness, of life and of death, of righteousness and of sin. We find cause and explanation of the mystery—in the imputation of sin to Him as man, and in the possession of righteousness as God; in the mysterious entwining of the girdle that encompassed Him with human infirmity, and drew around Him the might of Divinity.

Hence, as were it a law of our moral and spiritual being, we find that all grand and lofty minds, in order to help humanity forward, must labour, study, and suffer apparent loss. Sometimes we must even endure impoverishment, weakness, disease, if we will attain the highest mental and moral stage. The brilliancy of reason and imagination—so dazzling; the true humility, spotless purity, harmlessness of the dove—so hallowing; are wrought by patience in perfect work, with continual advance towards the ideal of a perfect human being. It is indeed something sad that, in our present state, the torch of a mind surpassingly splendid must attain the kindling, and retain the shine, from a pure flame of self-sacrifice. The inner courts of wisdom, the highest summits of purity, can only be attained by Christly-men. To have our spiritual and intellectual elements of character in perfect harmony, and that there be fullest development of both, we must walk on earth as that One walked who came from Heaven to make us Sons of God by supernatural selection.

Many thoughts arise in connection with so great a wonder; thoughts connected with the universe.

Our whole system of worlds, viewed so far as we can by the most powerful telescope, possibly does not bear so great a relation to the entire universe as a single leaf to all the leaves of a forest: nor are we to imagine that Nature copies herself accurately and incessantly throughout space. There are many worlds, why not many sorts? why not a variety rich and manifold as the Divine perfections? Jesus, by taking flesh in so small a world as ours, opens out a prospect into many spheres whence enraptured spirits behold the great transaction. The Incarnation is not merely the encompassing of the Infinite, so that the Incomprehensible may be possessed and embraced: it is the bringing into our earthly sphere, it is a closing within our human nature, that embodiment of the Holy and Mighty which conveys right and power to go through the gateways of sense, of intelligence, of emotion, to possess infinite and various glory. Talk no more of material beauties, of the worlds shrined in dew-drop, in miracles of splendour on butterfly-wing, they are as nothing to God manifest in the flesh; less than nothing to the glorious transformation and marvellous inner fashioning by which we are fitted to know and rejoice in the Almighty.

Again—We may be sure that law exists everywhere, we are not sure of uniformity. We listen to the voice of experience concerning natural order, and we hearken to wisdom as to distinguished exceptions, in the universe is room for all. What special union of streams in one or many places was needed for the bringing forth of light; what was manifested of the Unknown when the firmament was spread, and the boundaries of land and sea were arranged for perpetual variation; none can know. The peculiar nature infused when plant-life, beast-life, man-life, began to live—who can say? Every one was a true revelation, a real coming forth of the Absolute. There were curious intersections and interactions of energies on, round, in, and through substances, during years, ages, cycles: but in the first germ of plant, of beast, of man, there was true God-manifestation in various degrees; even as the Incarnation of Christ was a God-manifestation of excellent degree. Those rendered this possible, and this conferred on those highest meaning; adding to temporal life the gift of life everlasting. Pascal well said—"Who can do otherwise than admire and embrace a religion which contains the deep knowledge of truths: which we still know the better the more we receive."

The Nature and Work of Christ are preternatural and

supernatural, the Christ-life, and the Christ-death, transcend all other—enthrone Divinity of morality in the humanity of existence. We, for our part, do not see how we can account for a nature producing such marvellous moral results, or for the powers of a mind so greatly influencing the world, unless we allow that He possessed peculiar qualification as Healer of Souls, as Seer of things invisible, as a Spirit in communion with the Realities of the universe. Looking at Sin, looking at the Atonement; our science and intellect, our conviction and emotion, say—"Man hath sinned and God hath suffered."

If we recognize this as the initial process for Divine rectification of existing wrong, the remedy for prevailing wretchedness, we shall also recognize the work which is given us to do. Persistent sagacious efforts for the improvement of the moral and material condition of humanity on the earth, to be intellectually and morally right, to be spiritually, socially, and physically happy, conduce to welfare and honour in future life. When we so live in and by our Christianity, that with concentrated and urgent attention we transform, aye, transfigure the state of our land and people; so that wise simplicity, divine purity, gentle peace, and gladsomeness, possess our country; we shall know and possess the beginnings of that Good Time which was promised by Christ.

Take the pictures of early life darkly drawn by Sir John Lubbock, the investigations of Darwin, ancient and modern history, the common and uncommon facts of every life, and see whether a coming Salvation, which science in error calls " the progress and triumph of humanity," is not the grand truth which explains the mystery of creation, the mystery of evil, the mystery of miracle? The creation we understand, humanly, as a Revelation of Godhead bringing fashioned substance with forms of life and beauty out of chaos. The existence of evil we tremble at as caused by the voluntary faults of intelligent free creatures in rebellion against Supreme Holiness. The operation of miracle in Inspiration of the Bible, Incarnation, Resurrection, Ascension of Jesus, and Coming of the Holy Ghost, are a Divine amending of the fault, a Divinity of process by which our world will be restored and grandly embellished.

Creation, material and spiritual, can only be adequately understood when viewed as a display of the Almighty's attributes; and we must think of it—not from what is lowest but from that which is highest. The low cannot exceed their own level, and ascend to the high; but it is a property of the high that it can descend to the low, elevate, and make it partake of the descending greatness. The aspirations of men are not transformations of brutal passions into spiritual instincts, not dreams produced by indigestion, not illusions from the marshy ground of reptiles: they are the breathings in our intellect and emotion, finding utterance in our language, and embodiment in our acts, of that Holy Reality who gives substance, life, intelligence, and emotion to all His creatures. The Divine Narrative of Antiquity, concerning this, deserves reverence: as truth—it is the ground on which we stand; its progress, or unfolding, is a sure and perfect way for our feet; and on it we make the great progression to Higher Life.

It follows from all this, that Jesus is the great original moral Worker and Thinker—unique in the world. His comprehensiveness of character is rendered more wonderful by the consideration that His youth was spent in a small country town apart from the strife of politics, from the great questions of the age, and amongst the simplest and most uncultured of men. He was in no respect like the Roman, who aimed at establishing national supremacy by force of arms, to make Rome the eternal city. In no particular did He resemble the Greek, who sought to subdue the earth by culture, by art, by science, by literature, by philosophy. Far from embodying the aims and aspirations of His own countrymen, He was, and ever has been, so opposed to their peculiar mode of thinking and conduct of life, that the nation generally, even unto this day, refuses Him though He stands far ahead —the greatest and best of all Jewish men.

The marvel grows in connection with His birth, manner of life, peculiar genius, extraordinary death, when we remember that He was the foretold, the expected, the miraculous, the Blessed and Blessing One. He is all that now. His Advent; His glorious Reign—as the One True King; the praised and blessed of all, as He will be to the praise and blessing of all the true; is foretold and expected as the One Miracle more to crown and consummate all marvels. Now, while we wait, His beautifully shaped spoken thought awakes the slumbering human capacity into wonderful thought of sacred shaping power: so that the likeness of God is restored, while the Holy Ghost, within all spiritual men, gives beautiful grace and warmth to the whole by personal infusion and presence of Divine Love.

Jesus of Nazareth, by His touch of nature, not only maketh all the world akin; but, uniting in His own Person the excellences of our race and the grandeur of Divinity, is that Light which lighteth every man; and is that Personality whom true Positivists ought to acknowledge as Divine Humanity—the embodied Spirit of Progress.

By this Personality, Jesus is constituted the true King of the true Human Kingdom. He has done best of all men for science and morality, for liberty and truth. His Spirit was in Galileo, not in the persecutors; in Kepler and Newton, not in their maligners. He transmits influence from generation to generation, enabling disciples to imitate Him; and to be the progressive part of mankind. The centuries and nations without Him are silent. All the works that are now done in high faith, good hope, and true love; the smith, here, with that metal of his; and every craftsman with method of cunning; become sublime by the greater works, the love and faith and hope of Christ: He is the realization of our race. He made that noblest of all ideas, "Immortality," a real thing; and aggrandizes men into the happy capacity for it, infusing them with His nature, by means of their faith. All that we do and bring to pass in the way of advance, is by effectuation of His thought, and in realization of His polity.

In Christ all are alive, out of Christ all are dead. Our London—whatever is good in houses and palaces, in shops and traffic, in engines and ships, in churches and cathedrals, in the skilled and grand realities of modern life—is the embodiment of Divine thought in humanity—or human thought inspired by Him who is the Head of men. Who built Westminster Abbey? St. Paul's Cathedral? Look into the heart of the matter, it was that Divine Hebrew Man. His art was not artifice; yet, He was the great Artificer who, by means of thought, the mightiest thing that men possess, gathers around him the world's intelligence and emotion. To those who believe in Him as more than man, even to those who believe that He was an exceptional man, there is no great wonder in it. He, splendidly gifted, possessed everything possible to the limits of humanity; no one-sided development, but manifold perfectness. He was not only the greatest Thinker, but the greatest Realizer of thought. To Him, in all things we must attribute spiritual pre-eminence.

He meant, Jesus meant, that kings, priests, and all manner of persons, in public and private, should take His Word for their law; and be consciously under, willingly obedient to, the Government of God. The time will arrive, when His prayer—"Thy kingdom come"—shall be an established Dominion. Those who believe that so many ages of the past were needful to make man what he now is, ought to be the most patient in waiting, and diligent in working for the development of this grand scheme of Imperial Rule. We will all set our face toward our inheritance and home, prepare for our place amongst the ranks that encircle the Eternal Throne; not only nourish our own soul into the steady and enduring flame of a holy life, but carry many of our fellows with us to the threshold of that scene where the beholders never die. If we thus make our strenuous human efforts to be as a translation of His Will into action, great things may be done, and, it may be, soon done. O! for the more holiness and faith and effort that might suffice, for the instantaneous result: "He spake, and it was done; He commanded, and it stood fast."

Put the thought into another form:—What some people call "Moral Evolution," "Spiritual Progress," is really effectuation by the Word of God. This Word, as in Holy Writ, regards the intelligence of the world; this Word, as in Jesus, regards the life and emotion of the world. Each has a special work, yet in both specialities is unity. The Written Word gives a spirit of knowledge, and the knowledge is power; the Personal Word confers ability to rule—to rule by being in subjection. When the knowledge passes into power possessed by the masses who have become holy, when subjection to God has laid hold of righteous dominion, there will be a change—as if we became dwellers in a palace; and the palace not strange, but our own familiar home—beautified and enlarged: the Earth becoming a possession of the Saints under the true Emperor, described by Horace, to whom God had committed the task "of expiating past sin"; and "all creatures, from the archangel in Heaven to the worm on earth," as said by Edward Irving, "bearing witness unto Christ."

There is, we acknowledge, a light in men apart from Christ—a light flashing from natural character; but it is as light from a wandering star, whose progress we view with anxiety and alarm. There is an influence exercised by the world, but we do well to harden ourselves against it: an influence the very reverse of that experienced by Alcibiades as to Socrates—"I flee away as fast as possible that I may not sit down beside him, and grow old in listening to his talk; for this man has reduced me to feel the sentiment of blame, which I imagine no one could readily believe was in me; he alone inspires me with remorse and awe, for I feel in his presence my incapacity of refuting what he says, or of refusing to do what he directs." So would the world make us flee from Christ, but He wins and holds us; and is conquering the world itself: for His language, full of emotion, comes from the Heart of hearts, and as the Italians said of Dante—"Eccovi l' uom ch' è stato all' Inferno"—we say of Jesus: His words were molten in the fire of His heart, elaborated in His Divine intellect, and they came forth in intense earnestness, every one answering to the other in its own place, His Spirit going forth with them to make a world of heroes—men of His own moral image, bright and true, to be permanently and supremely glorious. Through Jesus we possess thoughts too mysterious and wonderful for utterance; a light of truth which brings Heaven within; and His love so enters our hearts that He is present in the thought, in the light, in the love, rendering indestructible every Word and all the Work. O, it is very wonderful! a miracle of miracles! the Uncreated, the Incomprehensible, the Invisible, the Deity embodied in human form, walking among men, partaking of their infirmities, leaning on their bosoms, weeping over their graves, slumbering in the manger, dying on the cross, rising from the grave. He, the world's Healer, Restorer,

Comforter, Glorifer of Humanity, says—"Come unto me, all ye that labour and are heavy laden, and I will give you rest. Take my yoke upon you, and learn of me; for I am meek and lowly in heart: and ye shall find rest unto your souls" (Matt. xi. 28, 29).

THOUGHT XXVI.

RESPICE, ASPICE, PROSPICE.

"Man is a little world, for all the mysteries of nature are treasured up in him."

RESPICE—We are sure, looking back upon our argument, that miracles, physical and moral, are verified, Nature is God Almighty's Garment, which He fashioned by Creation, which He uses in Providence. Those who tell us that to work a miracle, the Lord must derange and change the universe to utmost limits, may well be told—The will of man changes and conquers the course of nature, rendering every law submissive; if man does this without derangement of the universe, shall the Almighty be incompetent? We know, moreover, that Nature was not always complete, as to the past; nor is it now eternally complete for the future; it winneth evermore victories from chaos for life and beauty; we have seen but the smallest part of the Lord's Dominions.

Aspice—We look around, faith in God—in the Supernatural, is that bright star which guides into a safe haven. Miracles are sparks glistening on the wheel of Divine Providence as it revolves in ordinary work. They are probable, reasonable, natural, coming from

Him by whom nature exists; and Supernatural as controlling nature. Nature is afflicted with a fatal malady, and miracles are a part of the means, elixirs in the healing prescription of the great Physician. It is in the course of Nature that medicines heal; yet they entirely change the otherwise regular current of events, and bring in a new and endless range of consequent events; that, in place of death, life rules and man is saved. Hence it follows that things are not fated, we are not bound with a chain of inseparable links; there are insertions of variety, the links are not as if welded—they are magnetic links as under control of a Great Electrician, and are used for translation of Divine Will into natural effect and human effort, according to the wise counsel of our loving Father. History, art, science, all our experience, shows that the world is mysterious, wonderful, miraculous, in every part. We cannot fully know the cause or causes of any event—whether it is great or small; in origin, in continuance, in passing away, in the whole and in every fragment, the earth and our life on it are mysteries. We cannot tell what a moment may bring forth, but we know, in a manner not to be mistaken, that the Most High reigneth.

Prospice—Looking forward, we see that the anthropomorphism of our argument is not feebleness, but real strength. The counterpart of it is in the intelligible framework of the universe; and, we speak reverently, we must judge of God in accordance with the faculties which we possess, and the discerned government of nature. Moreover, we discern a likeness to the constitution of our own character in the texture of that Holy Mind, the Divine Incarnation, Jesus. All belonging to this Jesus—the prophecies, Birth, Life, Death, Resurrection, sending of the Holy Ghost—are such a Revelation of God that we may have knowledge of the Divine Nature, and power by it. Pascal says—"Non seulement nous ne connaissons Dieu que par J. C., mais nous ne connaissons nous mêmes que par J. C." Now, though trial and sorrow may come, we shall never part company with that Divinely given blessed heart-moving hope—"tremolar dell' onde"—that beautiful measured rhythm of the grand ocean's waves of Immortality connecting all the pure in heart to a Heavenly Home.

Miracles, as we look back, were the great steps by which nature ascended the heights of being and existence. As we look around, miracles are seen in all new life, and sustainment of old life; in the rhythm of all things, the current of electricity, the pulsation of life, and the throb of our breast; in the tidal-wave, succession of day and night, and in cycles of the universe. Mysterious invisible Will is everywhere producing effects without any known intermediate agencies. Miracles, as we look forward, are stars gleaming on our life's waves, which cause the surface of our mental ocean to sparkle with Divine iridescence. View the past, the present, the future; our conscience, our reason, our science, detect, accept, and approve miraculous working.

Not only so, in every land and language are records of marvels. Believers in them are not the credulous and rash, but the most intellectual and prudent of men. Human consciousness, growing up from the very root of things, is possessed with the conviction of Divinity by whom it grew; discerns the fact that all effects are from the Great Cause; and faith in the One Life that rose from among the dead, is no great difficulty to him who knows that all life was originally a rising out of the dead. The grain of wheat abideth alone, unconscious of all its surrounding; but if it die, if the warm prolific moisture of the settled furrow decomposes all but that little salient point, the embryo, it will start up and bear much fruit. The frost-bound bulb of the snowdrop is not dead but sleepeth. If the south wind blow there will be a putting on of lovely garments; then, too, the lily sheds its slough, and transforms into the most exquisite image of moral purity. To believe in this or that departure from Nature's usual course, is not unreasonable to him who knows that every law is straight, or circular, or spiral, or multiform; containing all varieties, conceivable and inconceivable eccentricities.

Forged miracles are not disproof, but proof of universal conviction as to the reality of the true. The statement that narratives of miracles chiefly abound among ignorant, barbarous, and credulous nations is not accurate: the most compact, continued, intelligible, and credible account is given by the most remarkable people in the world. All religion is based on conviction of the Supernatural, a miracle-stream flows through all history, and scientific measurement proves that it is deep and wide. If it be said—"Past experience can only be verified by cross-examination of the witnesses, which is impossible; and that belief in the Scripture miracles rests on our consciousness of fitness, rather than on demonstrations of their truth;" we reply—The moral consciousness of fitness is in itself a conviction that the experience of former men was veritable. Nor is that all: the miracles of Scripture are marvels exceeding all other wonders, are in connection with truths so vast, morality so pure, and men so grand, that the accusation of ignorance, barbarism, superstition, must be scornfully refused. They rest on past experience which can be verified, at least in part, by our own consciousness and conviction of supernatural power; and on present facts, which we may investigate. The experience was that of millions; and the present facts are those convictions of truth and righteousness, those convictions of sin and judgment, those feelings of love and awe, those feelings of immortal hope, which every true man is conscious of. These convictions and feelings are utterly delusive, unless they rest on objective supernatural realities. Thus resting, they themselves partake of the supernatural; or if they do not so rest, taking the other view, they are akin to the miraculous as being worldwide phenomena, for which, if you take away the realities giving them life, you cannot account. Or, if you do account, it is by spiritual miracles, and refusing those in physical matters, which is absurd: for the power displayed in old miracles is manifested in spiritual conversions day by day, in marvellous enlightenment, renewal of strength, abounding of joy.

Of all nations in the world, the Jews had highest knowledge of God, purest morality, the best and wisest laws. The miracles wrought among them were not for show; nor to obtain for the workers personal influence, power, and wealth; but for separation of the race from impure and godless nations, and to establish faith in One God. They were the most incredulous of all people, and received no marvels but those specially attested, connected with moral precept, civil and ecclesiastical law, the life and worship of the nation. If it be said—" Their continual idolatry before the Captivity, and their readiness at the Christian era to believe every impostor, prove their credulity;" we reply— The common sense of the nation always righted itself; these perturbations, trials, and experiences of other religions, and of asserted marvels, caused them to return with additional reverence and tenacity to the common faith. Only marvels recorded by public monuments and religious memorials are now received by them; and these form the nation's character, habits, literature, religion, aspirations, and science.

These marvels, we admit, are antecedently incredible and, to all appearance, utterly impossible; but, so soon as wrought and attested, they are confirmed and partly explained by natural similitudes. In addition, the fact of being wrought: I. in opposition to Evil and Error; II. in confirmation of Righteousness and Truth; yields peculiar and satisfying conviction.

I. Evil and error are indeed painful facts, and universal. There is not merely the dulness of error; but an appreciable cleverness in the manifested evil; indeed, a skill of the very highest subtlest kind in the various combinations of evil, physical and psychical, mental and moral. Satanic craftiness and inhuman malice, against God and holiness, as an intricately devised and elaborately executed maze of iniquity, mix with the whole course of history; and, with crooked ramifications, perverts human and all other life—making the whole earth to groan. This evil, moreover, is connected with strangest mythologies, idolatry, spirit-culture, and devil worship; is affirmed to be allied with an Evil Principle asserting himself in marvels — diabolically wrought, inciting men to selfishness and sensuality, obscenity and superstition. It is that which creates the greatest difficulty as to faith in the existence and personality of God: it seems to deny the omnipotence, omniscience, and beneficence of the Supreme.

As a warning against, and a means of resisting and overcoming, the evil, Holy Scripture was given, and Divine miracles were wrought. The people unto whom Scripture was given, and amongst whom the miracles were performed, were separated from the idolatrous mysteries and wonder-workers of other nations. A pure ritual and holy laws, a wonderful system of morals and doctrine, enabled them to attain the highest development of morality in the world. The prophets, by whose Inspiration and God-given power, came the Revelation and Might, were men who lived for the honour and service of the One Holy Lord. It is not possible, nor credible, that these men should lie and deceive in the name of that Holy One; that tricks of jugglery should be passed off as miracles by men of purest morality, and in connection with the grandest and most spiritual doctrines of which the world has ever obtained knowledge.

No sane man regards such a horrible thing as possible or credible; the worst and most immoral of unbelievers allow that the Apostles, and those after them, honestly believed what they related—though mistaken in that belief. The plea of mistake, of error, will not avail. The writers of the Old Testament, of the Gospels, of the Acts, of the Epistles, of the Revelation, declare, as a fact, that they themselves had performed miracles, had seen, known, and tested, the reality of miraculous works, and were ready to die in witness of their truth.

It is a confirmation of the previous arguments, that Satanic—possibly pretended—miracles, preceded the Scripture marvels; that ignorance and superstition have hollowed a channel for a stream of diabolical delusions to run through the whole course of human history and life. Indeed, the existence, or asserted existence, of these evil marvels accounts for the surprisingly little influence exercised by real miracles: the Jews, in many instances, not being persuaded however great the wonders that were wrought. Some of the holiest men, however, have honestly believed in "ecclesiastical miracles," which we know were delusions; and men of highest intelligence have believed in Witchcraft. On this account, Revelation appeals, rather, to common sense than high-mindedness; to holiness, to truth, rather than the abnormal scepticism of morbid intellectuality; and only in contending with malice and unbelief—more than human, and a more than world-power craftily sustained by stupendous signs, are miracles wrought. Christ positively refused to work any miracle for the conviction of unbelievers. This shows that an opponent has no warrant for saying—"Revelation rests upon miracles, and miracles rest only upon Revelation, therefore, I reject them both:" for the argument, as to Christianity, is not so much that we are to receive it because of the marvels, but that the sublime mind, perfect purity, and far-sighted sagacity of the Saviour could not possibly have allied Himself or His Gospel to a lie. It is equally impossible that men who loved Him for His truth, who died on behalf of it, and in maintenance of His holiness, could have distorted His life and defiled His teaching; or could have lived in falsity, and died traitors against His purity.

II. Miracles obtain verification of a peculiarly convincing character, when viewed in connection with the wide plan, profound doctrines, and holy precepts of Christ.

The plan embraces all time, all men, all earthly things, and is asserted to be mysteriously linked with intelligences and operations in other worlds. It proposes and undertakes the abolition of evil, the establishment of purity, and the raising of all things to a higher stage of being and existence. As it is a part of this plan to act by moral and loving persuasion on behalf of right, purity, and truth, Revelation and Miracles are launched with only so much force as is necessary to win and maintain their acceptance by the pure-minded; in nowise to coerce the wilful unbeliever, or to compel the wicked and malicious. When conversion to holiness has been wrought by a consideration and knowledge of God's Plan of Salvation; when love enters the heart, and constrains the affections to forsake sin; then miracles are the seal of God that the Truth is indeed Divine. The men thus won, seem then to receive an exaltation and vividness of cerebral faculties amounting almost to a new sense. It is not "religiosity," it is not a preternatural exaltation of imagination, not a goading of the mind to an unnatural state of susceptibility; but we call it "specifically spiritual." A power, a vividness, a purity, a far-sightedness, such as possess men who say on the approach of their dissolution—"Many things are growing clear to us."

The doctrines in connection with miracles, are not less wonderful. They declare that the Evil Principle, causing alienation from God, will be destroyed by the Good Principle, the Personal God, imparting His own Nature to 'the flesh of men; that thus man shall be made Divine, and the Earth become a Paradise. This great doctrine of Incarnation includes all other sacred mysteries, explains and renders them possible. It has threefold illustration: 1. Nature, as seen in Creation, is a material phenomenon, or embodiment; 2. Literature, as represented in Holy Scripture, is an intellectual phenomenon, or embodiment; 3. Man, as he stood in Eden —a living soul, and man as he stands by new birth in Christ—a quickening spirit, are the living, the physical, the spiritual phenomena. Thus, there are three Revelations of the Almighty: a Material Universe, an Inspired Book, an Incarnate God-man. Every one of these Revelations displays two powers contending for supremacy: Good and Evil; and they are all bound up into a plan or scheme of twofold development; individual perfection of every creature, and perfection of the universe. We, who are men, must individually do our work: raise the masses to that high standard of harmonious human virtue and capacity which will enable them to receive glorious inspiration from the Almighty, and habitually to walk in the light of His countenance. To men thus perfected will come a perfect life, and a regenerated earth (Rev. xxi. 1-4). Then, with the relish of an unspoiled nature, with the fulness of a wise spirit, with the emotion of a thankful heart, we shall partake in blissful serenity of those good things which surpass all our present understanding.

The precepts, in connection with miracles, are an affirmation of verity: they carry human conduct into very sublimity of life, by representing Godly height as the true and possible stature and attainment of man. The process of elevation is wrought by that revelation of God in Nature, in Holy Scripture, in Christ, which, becoming intelligently approved by the human will and planted in the affections, elevates the will and affections into capacity to investigate, ascertain, and appreciate the true nature and blessed power of supernatural exhibitions. Men thus selected, with minds thus elevated, were chosen to be Inspired Writers; and, in general, to be witnesses of miracles; and they unquestionably, through their far-sightedness and purity, exercised and still exercise a sacred influence on the customs, literature, and science of the world. Those nations who have not yielded faith to the miracles, and their life to be guided by the doctrines of Scripture, are the weakest, poorest, and of least avail for good, in the Earth. As to individuals, it is found that every man who refuses the Bible and its miracles is without a well-founded hope of immortality, remains in gross darkness even as to Divine Personal Existence, and finds the mysteries of life wholly inexplicable.

The conclusion at which we arrive—after reviewing the past, regarding the present, and considering the future—is: that Miracles being attested by men who were Inspired to be Prophets, and Workers for God, are worthy of all acceptation; the Scriptures, themselves, not being the least of the miracles. We are furthermore persuaded, that Evil and Error rendering miracles necessary, true miracles are separated from Satanic marvels, and affirmed to be Divine Workmanship, by their connection with a wonderful plan of Salvation, marvellous doctrines, and holy precepts. The Infinite God, moreover, who is beyond nature, is the Creator of nature; and, however inconceivable, and unexplainable in terms of physical science, He so reveals Himself to us, by means of Nature, that our inner man is in some way a far-off shadow of His own Being; while all the gentlest and beautifulest of our emotions lead us to believe that we are children of His love, whom He is leading to a Heavenly Land. Science does indeed show that the world is not only mechanical but vital, intellectual, spiritual. It is not a world that any present mechanical system can explain: but it is certainly a world in which every man needs to pray—" Guide me aright, strengthen me to do good, deliver me from evil." The existence of such a world, our freedom in it and responsibility, our need of moral guidance, the gift of strength, our preservation from evil, are only possible, and we may even say useful and intelligible, as parts of a vast comprehensive teleological plan of Divine Government. A plan which, while affording scope for all the activities of freedom, controls that freedom by presenting to the intellect and emotion such indications of loving Might and Wisdom, in opposition to all evil, as content the pure desires of our inner man; and bring back the various intelligences to that loving voluntary obedience from which evil had caused them to wander. Such a plan, in the whole and in every part, is essentially miraculous.

THOUGHT XXVII.

ONE MIRACLE MORE.

" There is a history in all men's lives
 Figuring the nature of the time deceased;
 The which observ'd, a man may prophesy,
 With a near aim, of the main chance of things,
 As yet not come to life, which in their seeds
 And weak beginnings lie intreasured."
                SHAKESPEARE, *Henry IV., Part II.*

CONVICTION that moral scepticism is spiritual paralysis, fated to end in misery, brings in another Thought concerning a further miracle.

Christ came to bring healing for the black malady. He does not forbid our being bold inquirers, or even sceptical reasoners, about finite things of the present or of the past; but He invites our wonder, our love, our exultation, about the infinite, the unseen, the future. He would have us glory in faith, in thanksgiving, in obedience, in worship, as to the Supreme. Look at the men apart from Christ if you would know the work He has to do. Some, through scepticism, discern nothing but mechanism in the world; and altogether miss the wonderful open secret. Witchcraft is better. Carlyle says—" Witchcraft worshipped at least a living devil; but this worships a dead iron devil." Other men are even worse; for ever seeking pleasure, always in fear of pain; they are not far removed from the miserables whom Satan roasts at great fires of delusion, while the cheat and knave, chartered by him, eat, drink, and are merry. Merest trivialities of all are the light-chafers and fire-flies, flickering in the ways of sin, whom the Evil One, by piercings of their own lust, affixes to iniquities. Of poor creatures like these, with nothing good in them, Christ could make something; but they resist with all their might. The best of these sceptics, who honestly thinks that it is a large part of the business of the wise to counteract the efforts of the good; who says—"the greater the knowledge, the greater the doubt;" even this, the chief man, admits that the deeper he goes the less easy it is to obtain soundings, and, while doubtful as to being right himself, is sure that all the ancient saints were wrong. Such a man cannot be accounted happy. If he has any senses of the soul, he distrusts them; and seems to possess no power of living as one who sees Him who is invisible; nor has he that kind of nerve and brain which realizes the ineffable mysteries of the Divine Presence and of the Unseen World. Alas! for the men who, boasting of finest intellect, thus "eat dirt."

Would any be an able man—the true nobleman, a man of worth—that is of worship, would he have faculty to be a knowing one—the king-man, let him go to Christ for that spirituality which gives light and power to the intellectual faculties. Those who think that they can make a good time on the earth, by levelling all the great men to the immensity of little men's low degree;

will of course prattle about blessed equality—being so silly as not to know that it is impossible to find one wise man in a host of innumerable foolish creatures. If let alone, they would yet more diminish themselves; but Christ, by His Doctrine and Spirit, gives them—despite their unbelief, a capacity to possess powers by which they lay hold of the world to come. Then, possessing this Divine influence, they may, if they will, think out, act out, and become a blessing to themselves and to their country. When all men are thus influenced and empowered, there will be the reign spoken of by science as the kingdom of man. Scripture more truly calls it the Kingdom of Christ, and Reign of the Saints.

On first looking out from our heart into the night, scepticism seems a pall of darkness enshrouding a dead world; but, more intently viewing the great vault of immensity, we learn to trust Him who supports all that, and are comforted. The design of the Designer does not begin at the end instead of the beginning. His plan of progression includes a race of rational beings, who pass through gradations from the Australian to a Newton. Ploughed with this thought, the earth becomes a very harvest-field, where the yellow corn bending every golden head is figure of the Bread of God that comes down from Heaven, and our soul's sustenance is felt to be very nigh. Everything brings a lesson—"That little bird," said Luther, "above it are the stars and deep heaven of worlds; yet its little wings are folded; it goes trustfully to rest in its home —the Maker has given it a home." We too have a Home. When our sojourning and wayfaring are accomplished, we shall be at Home in our Father's House.

We cannot avoid thinking of our Home, and why should we try? The thought is fascinating and maintainable, makes us happier, better, wiser men. Looking upon living things, we behold them passing into death; whence, as if to fulfil the yearnings of our heart, they issue in new forms of being and existence—proving that death is change, not destruction. The component elements of every organism are separated and dissipated; metals and rocks dissolve, little by little, into thin air; it is only to be re-formed—nothing is lost. The sun, flooding the hills with splendour, wastes no sparklet nor ray of light. Nature does not pour forth her brightest smiles upon our countenance, and then deceitfully bear us to realms of outer darkness. We are not sparks and flashes merely betokening that natural heat which endureth but for a moment: what does the moral stage denote, unless it be a sign and proof that man is an immortal being? Our dying, and we die daily, is for renewal of the living substance; and, so dying, behold, we live! This miracle of life ought to be more fully proclaimed by men of science. They ought to tell us plainly, that in the proportion we neglect our intellectual and devotional faculties we thwart and traverse our destiny; and mar even our physical welfare. The present time and place and state are a ground-plan for future variety; and as all life came from precedent life, intelligence from higher Intelligence, our personality from an essential Person; so our life, intelligence, and personality—capable of a degree of elevation and perfection, the attainment of which on earth seems almost impossible, as they cannot be meant to remain for ever in an imperfectly developed state—pass on into the wider life, greater intelligence, wonderful personality, which are our glorious future heritage.

Indestructibility is not the attribute of matter only: our power of thought, of love, of virtue, of progressive holiness, are better things; and the better do not die while the worse live on. These better, in fact, are the cause of harmonious development in all, enriching even the physical organization. Those worse we take up, as it were, from the ground; the better we take, so to speak, from heaven; thus we belong to two worlds—pilgrims through the present unto permanent dwellings in the future. We combine in the mortal body the inorganic and organic substance of the universe, resemble the lowest animals; yet excel the highest in the wonders of our sensational, intellectual, and emotional life. If we develop all the elements of our nature earthly perfection will ultimately adorn our earthly destiny; and the full height of spiritual and intellectual culture enable every man to say, " In God I live, and move, and have my being." In our frame is exhibited the direct action of spirit on matter—a continual miracle—turning the dull, cold, insensate clods of earth into bright, warm, intelligent existence: day by day we may be said to glorify the lower world, bringing it within the reach and range of mental and spiritual capacity, so that we are fellow-workers of the Most High. This re-creation has another and a higher counterpart. Our natural person becomes a spiritual person: not only by imitating those grand types and patterns of men which God gave in early history, we are now influenced by Christ's Person—the God-man's nature, we are won to high living conscious union with God, who dwells in our own substance. It was before this Deity, shrined in a human form, walking among men, partaking of their infirmities, reclining on their bosoms, weeping over their graves, bleeding on the cross, that the prejudice of the Jew, the scepticism of the Greek, and the pride of the Roman, were humbled in the dust. He touches us, He handles; we, meanwhile, seeing, knowing, feeling the fashioning, are re-moulded—made new men; and, by this process of spiritual creation, pass into the Divine Nature which has come down into ours; and enter Divine Life that we, not on earth only, but in grander spheres, may represent the wonder and beauty of this Christly process—the advance, the elevation, the perfection of Humanity.

The Christly process is greatly hindered by unbelief. Because of this unbelief, Christ can as yet do none of His greatest works. Even miracles are not believed in by some, though the earth is full of them, and the stars shine with them, and the sun sends heat through them, and all life lives in them, and all intelligence brightens by them. They want miracles that enforce faith, enchain reason, coerce affection, compel conscience: forgetting that for God so to work, and for miracles so to impel, there would be no human co-operation with the Divine, no response of will—of love—of intelligence—to holy motions. Let those men of science who abuse their high position, and misuse their knowledge, take to heart the fact, that the Christly process is essentially moral, peculiarly spiritual, intensely voluntary, in all on whom it is to be wrought. Let them aim at child-like trust in the Great Father, let them walk in the steps of His Holy Son, let them ask for the influence of the Eternal Spirit, and all true saving doctrine shall come into them, as the fruit of that doing, to be the seed of works yet more wonderful. In doing this, they will find a cure for unbelief; find that in their own small sphere they are demiurges, or little gods, able to do much. Though they may be soon tired, they will discern deep marks of human progress. This, we say, will be a cure for unbelief; because they will discern that they themselves being forces and causes in the cosmos, it is no diminution to the majesty of One Eternal Will that there should be many other free but finite powers, who arrange their forces in our little planet; and some for good, and some for evil; so that it is easy to understand why so much is mischievous, and grievously out of harmony. One part of the Lord's beneficent design is to subdue and sanctify the human will; after that all things are to be made new (Acts iii. 21).

The Christly process has been refused, and is still resisted, by the race chosen to manifest Christ's Person; and through their unfaith, continued and confirmed by our own unwisdom, want of zeal and love, two-thirds of mankind remain untouched by the Divine consecration. We present no theory, not even a guess, as to the reason or purpose of this; but if we call to mind the length of past time during which we have been in continuous development as conscious beings; and then recollect the vast period occupied in fitting the earth to become our dwelling, we shall find firm ground, even in the difficulty itself, for faith that it is a mysterious part in some grand process; and that when we have attained our improved condition we shall look back in remembrance of this, and know even as we are known. The Supreme must be indeed Almighty, for none but He could conceive and perform so wonderful a redemption. His Work must prevail; but at present it is hindered by man, and marred by Satan. It is time that our spirit cease to strive against Him who seeks to do us good, that we be willing and obedient.

The Christly process has also been hindered by an Evil Principle of stupendous power. Nothing less than such a Spirit of Evil can account for nature's evils, man's iniquities, and the comparatively little fruit resulting from the glorious Gospel. We find evil woven into all things by a plan most intricate and elaborate: matter, and all its elements; life, and all its sensations; intelligence, and all its thoughts; conscience, and all its emotions; are subject to a process by which good is marred, life is slain, intelligence is degraded, and the conscience is defiled. The evil is rooted in the foundation of the earth, grew up with it, and is now in every part. It could not originate in inert matter, was not life's fault, nor an error of human intelligence: for it is an active spirit, was manifested before life began, and took advantage of human intelligence—so soon as human intelligence existed. The mental history of mankind presents few sadder spectacles than is afforded by the convulsive contortions, the almost incredible feats of ingenuity performed by unbelief in order to liberate itself from this torture-chamber of the soul. Thousands have charged Infinite Goodness and Illimitable Power with the creation of evil. Thousands have made shipwreck of their faith, truthfulness, life, by wilfully yielding to evil—not manfully resisting it. Nevertheless, the problem is not wholly insoluble by humanity. If we assume—and indeed we know—that there is freedom in our world, and freedom in the universe, and that by grievous error evil was chosen rather than good, light breaks in. Indeed, the only explanation afforded by matured thought is: one or more free beings must, in some world preceding our own, have departed by wilful disobedience from uprightness; and in course of time that evil extended to our earth in· its substance, its life, its intelligence, its conscience. The lower manifestations in the earth being, not only the fruit of the past, but the seed of the future; and a means of awful degradation to the lowest depths of being and existence.

This evil is not an essential part of the Divine Plan: indeed, is no part of it, is opposed to it, and can only be explained as caused by the wilful error of free responsible creatures: otherwise, God is author of evil, which is absurd; for, in that case, He would act against Himself. We make half our difficulties, as to the mystery, by misunderstanding the word "Omnipotent." If God gives freedom, as a real gift, all consequences must be included; and that freedom may be free not even the evils, if foreseen, can be overruled except by presenting to the free erring creatures moral, not physical persuasion; for voluntary acceptance, not coercive enforcement. It is not well to say—"God cannot;" but we know that God will not depart from those limitations and conditions which His own Wisdom imposes upon His own Might. We cannot deny the sorrowful events which surround our life, but it is greatly in our power to ameliorate them for ourselves and for others; and when we worship God we well know that whether in allowing evil, or taking evil away, He will not act in opposition to our own moral sense. Glorification of all things, beatification of every intelligence, may be fairly placed amongst the essentials; but evil, as the product of freedom in rebellion, could not be a matter of fate; and, though foreseen, was not in the Almighty's plan, but against it; otherwise freedom were not freedom. Evil, then, being abnormal—not finding a remedy in the original constitution of things—necessitated new and further displays of Divine wisdom and mercy and might. These, so far as we are concerned, find expression in Christ, the Lamb of God, being appointed before the foundation of the world as the Divine Sacrifice for Sin; and they become Revelation to us in Holy Scripture; and they become part of our life in that all-embracing providential scheme which, little by little, is conducting our earth to a greater than the original good; the whole spiritual process allowing and securing perfect freedom to responsible intelligence. If science has a new Gospel; a better remedial, all-embracing, providential scheme, for the removal of deception and degradation from mankind, we will reverentially listen.

Meanwhile, we wait for that one miracle more completing all present miracles: bringing the world and worlds into a state so refined that the dust of our streets shall be dust of gold. The one miracle more is a trinity in unity: a glorification of nature, of life, of intelligence. The present earth is a microphone: its sounds, that we thought were stilled, reverberate—even the little ones —for ever. He who stealthily walks in sin, that his footsteps fall light as the tread of a fly, will find every one loud as war-horse tramp. He who, doing good, telleth not to left-hand what the right performs, shall have the good proclaimed for universal renown. In all matter, in all life, in all intelligence, are seeds; that everything may, according to its kind, produce a better and purer sort. Everywhere is involution, everywhere is evolution. Matter—in crystalline form, or in crystals —entering, as ground substance, into life; or moulded into receptacles for intelligence—may be considered as passing from the inorganic to the organic, from life to intelligence, by successive miraculous transitions. Streams that lisp to the stones, leaves that talk to the breeze, the ocean looking at the sun through the face of gleaming waves, the whole earth as a chariot of God, will enter life—be made of solemn beauty, a glorious living thing full of love and bliss—as by transaction of fire.

Life—so warm, so active, so sensitive, so low, so high, so minute, so majestic, of which the microscopic points may be far higher and grander than the middle term: life—reaching down from Him, in whom all life is, to that in which life is as though it were not; shall quicken and glorify in every rhythm till the universe is quick with the life of God. The low life working blindly into sight; dead life warming into lively glow; the structureless gaining structure; the indifferentiated winning differentiation of part for particular and special use; limbs and head, eye, mouth, ear, growing into highest form and use from that which had no figure nor function; all these are miracles of vitality. There may be crowns of material splendour, there may be trees of unfading beauty, there may be pavements of emerald, canopies of brightest radiance, gardens of loveliness, palaces of proud and stately decoration, with rivers flowing in unceasing gladness, but these are only the small parts of our bliss. One trembles at the Divinity in the Old Book declaring that all we men, being tried and purified, are from the ground; and one rejoices in the fact that science has found it true. Our fear and our joy make us better men. Oh, to think that the fins of the fish are the limbs of the lizard and parts of the bird by a Divinely wonderful advance! Then those other marvels, when we trace the eye, the ear, the mouth, the brain, from rudiments in creatures only beginning to be; so that eye, ear, mouth, brain, are in adjustment with an outer world of light—of sound—of flavours—of intricate design—all so interwoven with action and counteraction, equilibrium and ceaseless activity, that only Might everywhere, only Wisdom everywhere, only Life everywhere, are the due correlation of a universe so miraculously wonderful!

Intelligence—so clear, far-sighted, all-revealing—the light of God. By it we overtake suns and stars, with swifter velocity surpass their speed, with more might subdue their course, by measurement define their limits. It is the bright ladder of our ascent from grade to grade of being, from height to height of understanding, from world to world of existence, from the corporeal to the spiritual, from the natural to the Supernatural, from the creature to the Creator, from time to Eternity, from space to Infinitude. As the ascent, so the descent:

from man downward—ever and ever lower, through animal figures, through vegetal forms, through crystal shapes, to the amorphous and structureless, to a lesser shining and ever less, until in nothingness darkness finds abode. Only there, only in nothingness: so soon as the invisible becomes visible—aye before; so soon as the structureless takes structure, and organism is woven by life, aye before; intelligent work is manifested—the work of preceding intelligence. In every earth and metal, in every crystal and grass-blade, in phosphorescent gleam, in the darklings of creatures not yet created, in the sparklings of instinct, in the clearer and more continuous light illuminating the space between brute-reason and human understanding, and onward to the radiance of blessed genius, piety, and the bestowal of every power in use of the Holy One, through all the course and in every part, we trace the mind—the will—the operation of God—the Supreme Intelligence. Supreme Intelligence not working without the co-operation, intervention, and translation of our own human effort. A will here, a thought there, a word to this, a deed for that; so we become His agents on earth, and shall be made His angels in Heaven. O! thou man, toiling in humble drudgery, toil on as were thy toil a joy. O! thoughtful, anxious, troubled soul, look not so continually on the ground: draw a direct stream from the everlasting hills, through the channels of love and contemplation. O! you that are in darkness, can you not, in that darkness, discern a reason for seeking light in the fulness of the Creator, in the spiritual glories of the Holy and Perfect God? Strive to be of character kindred to His own, endeavour to restore the lost image of the Godhead in you, delight in prayer, and let your imagination kindle in beatific foretaste of Heaven. So shall you be fitted for glorious service : there may be missions of mercy to rescue the perishing—who knows? The despairing may have still to be reached, of missions consolation may yet be formed, and you go forth to instruct, to fight and conquer evil, and guide even worlds out of darkness into marvellous light. A miraculous work—a wonderful, thrilling, glorious destiny !

The Mystery of Miracles is unfolded so far as the poor mind of the thinker and writer can find idea and give expression. May He, in whose Name and for whose Honour it is written, graciously own the work. May those, for whose help it is penned, forgive the writer's weakness, shortcomings, and errors, for the work's sake ; be led to see that the mass of earth and worlds, the texture of all being and of every existence, are a marvellous building by the Almighty : that within these, within "the poor fragments all of this low earth," are being traced and formed more delicate and more spiritual forms, by means of Spiritual operation ; that the spirits of holy men, prophets, apostles, martyrs, sacred thinkers, holy doers, are the stones—the shafts —the columns—the walls and the head-stone—built into oneness with Christ's own Humanity, to be the Glorious Cathedral of God Almighty. The leaves of the Book of Existence turn slowly, one whole lifetime can hardly catch the meaning of a word in a sentence, in a page of universal being. However closely and intricately written, with imperceptible growth and unfolding of meaning, we read enough to discern that our every act of good or ill has its own work and place in God Almighty's plan; and, day by day, we resume our labour conscious of a dignity—sure of a destiny supremely glorious! We shall meet in the presence of our brethren.

THE END.

Woodfall & Kinder, Printers, Milford Lane, Strand, London, W.C.

BY THE SAME AUTHOR.

Demy 8vo., price 14*s.*

THE SUPERNATURAL IN NATURE,

A Verification by Free Use of Science.

CONTENTS.

I. IS INTELLECT DIVORCED FROM PIETY?
II. THE SUPERNATURAL.
III. THE THRESHOLD OF CREATION.
IV. RUDIMENTS OF THE WORLD.
V. ORIGIN OF LIFE AND THEORY OF RULE.
VI. CREATIVE WORDS.
VII. INTERPRETATION OF THE DAYS.
VIII. LIGHT.
IX. THE FIRMAMENT.
X. THE HABITATION OF LIFE.
XI. CREATION OF PLANTS.
XII. THE SUN.
XIII. FISHES, REPTILES, BIRDS.
XIV. CREEPING THINGS, BEAST, CATTLE.
XV. TWO DIVINE ACCOUNTS.
XVI. THE ADAMITE WORLD.
XVII. MAN—ORIGIN, NATURE, LANGUAGE, CIVILIZATION.
XVIII. HUMAN LIFE.
XIX. THE INVISIBLE.
XX. VARIETY IN NATURE.
XXI. FOLLIES OF THE WISE.
XXII. KINGDOM OF GOD.

"A book calculated to do much good. . . Care and research are manifest on every page. . . A really great work."—*The Bishop of Gloucester and Bristol.*

"I do not know any work which I could more willingly recommend to students of Theology and to the younger clergy, for their use in dealing with questions of physics in their relation to Revealed Truth."—*The Bishop of Lincoln.*

"Its great learning is only equalled by the variety and copiousness of the illustrations by which it is recommended to the reader. I never met with a work in which so many rays of light, from so many sources, and with such effect, were brought to bear upon the difficult questions taken in hand."—*J. A. Hessey, D.C.L., Archdeacon of Middlesex, &c., &c.*

"This thoughtful and elaborate work treats of many of the scientific problems or puzzles of the day in a very able manner. Throughout the whole of his work, even on those points wherein some thoughtful readers would dissent from him, there is a reverential spirit displayed which is as wide as the poles asunder from the vulgar flippancy which imagines that what each questioner of the Sacred Record imagines he can understand is the correlative of omniscience."—*Record.*

" Il y a peu d'ouvrages qui puissent être comparés au volume dont je voudrais donner ici une légère idée. L'auteur s'est préparé à sa tâche par de fortes études dans les différents cantons de la science. Il est également solide, quand il s'addresse à la métaphysique et quand il décrit la succession des époques en géologie, ou qu'il compare la texte de la Genèse avec celui des inscriptions conéiformes ; excellent hébraïsant, ses vues sur l'origine du langage sont aussi profondes qu'ingénieuses. Espérons, sans trop y conter, que l'excellent volume publié sous le titre de 'The Supernatural in Nature' servira à rectifier bien des erreurs, à détruire bien des préjugés, et à ramener à la foi bien des âmes qu'une fausse science en avait éloignées."—*Revue Bibliographique Universelle.*

"I cannot sufficiently express my sense of its value, especially in our day and country. . . It covers ground which no apologetic work hitherto published, so far as I know, at all attempts."—*H. P. Liddon, D.D., Canon of St. Paul's, &c., &c.*

" Great variety of illustration. . . Considerable cogency of reasoning. . . Not a little eloquence. . . A learned and instructive book . . To show that the deeper study of nature, in every field of inquiry, prompts and points to the recognition of the Supernatural."—*Contemporary Review.*

"The author has qualified himself by long and loving research, and by intimate acquaintance with the facts, principles, and advances of modern science. . . The volume abounds in glowing vistas, and is affluent with illustrations drawn from every department of literature and science. . . Altogether helpful and sunny. . . He demonstrates with extraordinary fulness of detail and illustration that at the door of every atom; and in the inviolable distinctions, the inconceivable velocities and innumerable vibrations of every molecule; in the infinitely numerous differentiations of the life germs, and, once more, in all the phenomena of mind; we are spectators, subjects, and recipients of the infinite eternal FORCE, which fills and actuates the unseen universe. . . The nature of miracle is discussed with much scientific force, and admirable replies to numerous sophisms are briefly given. . . A remarkable and interesting volume."—*British Quarterly Review.*

"This book displays a great deal of well-digested reading. . . Much curiously-gathered information upon all the questions on the present frontier of science."—*Academy.*

"Sufficiently remarkable, from its earnestness of tone, its wealth of scientific illustration, and the attractions of its style, to call for special notice. . . The book is exceedingly pleasant and readable. . . It is a work which will delight, and even instruct and elevate a large class of readers."—*Spectator.*

"We have long wished for such a work as this. So far from shrinking from the discoveries of modern science, it takes them up, acknowledges their value, and shows in the clearest manner that, instead of controverting the words of Scripture, they are perfectly consistent with them."—*National Church.*

"A most interesting and thoughtful book. . . The writer is evidently a good physicist and a capital naturalist, and well read in the literature of the subjects of which he treats; for the book bristles with quotations from a vast number of authors. . . In style the work is nervous and powerful, and not without a considerable amount of poetry of idea and diction. Here and there amongst the quotations we find flashes of wit and humour which tend to brighten the subject and amuse the reader."—*Literary Churchman.*

" A scholarly and reverent handling of a very difficult subject. . . It is due to the author to acknowledge the thoroughness and completeness of his scientific summary; he has neglected nothing, and he has suppressed nothing, however it may superficially tell against himself. . . The book is full of interest as a collection of scientific facts bearing upon the most momentous interests of man's life here and hereafter."—*Nonconformist.*

" The matter of this book is very good. . . The studies are exceedingly thoughtful and richly suggestive . . of intrinsic value . . indisputable power of thought, and wealth of knowledge and illustration."—*Liverpool Albion.*

" Its chapters abound in the proof of wide reading and a large acquaintance with all the branches of natural science; and both its reasonings and its conclusions will be welcomed by the believer in the inspiration of the Sacred Records. . . We accept with thankfulness and warmly commend this volume as a valuable permanent addition to our libraries, and as in many respects a storehouse of defensive armour against the assaults of materialists and other unbelievers. . . We are glad to commend the whole book to those readers who desire to have an answer ready against the suggestions of modern unbelievers. It will form a very storehouse for their purpose."
—*John Bull.*

C. KEGAN PAUL & CO.

1, PATERNOSTER SQUARE, LONDON, E.C.

www.ingramcontent.com/pod-product-compliance
Lightning Source LLC
Chambersburg PA
CBHW052213240426
43670CB00037B/440